T0146413

BERDICHEV TO BASILDON

ERIC MOONMAN

authorHOUSE®

AuthorHouse™
1663 Liberty Drive
Bloomington, IN 47403
www.authorhouse.com
Phone: 1 (800) 839-8640

Published by AuthorHouse 06/21/2017

ISBN: 978-1-5246-8506-5 (sc)
ISBN: 978-1-5246-8504-1 (hc)
ISBN: 978-1-5246-8505-8 (e)

Library of Congress Control Number: 2017905461

Print information available on the last page.

FOREWORD

"This is a timely book. There is much discussion in the media and parliament concerning the shortcomings of contemporary society and limited opportunities for the young and unqualified.

Time and again I have encountered policy makers urging that more should be done to help those in the working class. Perhaps some will be surprised to know that gaps still exist affecting youngsters who fall by the wayside and who lack access to pathways which would help them to achieve their potential and self justification.

Eric Moonman's account of a person without advantages yet who progressed with minimal education (having left school at thirteen) serving a seven year craft apprenticeship and developing in often difficult circumstances to emerge as an active and influential Member of Parliament is a fine example of tenacity and determination.

The author's adventures are remarkable but should not be considered unique. Others, with equally limited opportunities must take heart from Eric's achievements.

However, it is essential that the young are focused. In the author's case he worked and established for the International Red Cross, in Namibia, a three year economic and management system, which helped him in turn understand the value of, and enabled him to provide, mentoring to the next generation.

Eric Moonman has never been afraid to express his opinion. He was one of the first to establish a coordinated campaign in parliament supporting mental health.

I know that at times he was the bane of the government's whips office but was well respected by a former chief whip.

Beyond the Commons he has also been a great social campaigner and now we have the opportunity to understand his thoughts on society in the pages of his latest book.

Unlike any other political memoir the author's sense of humour and lightness of touch shine through.

A pleasure to read.

The Lord Hoyle

Also by Eric Moonman

The Manager and the Organisation (Tavistock, 221pp, Paperback edition Pan)

Communications in an Expanding Organisation (Tavistock)

Reluctant Partnership - a critique of Government Industrial Relations (Gollancz)

Industrial Innovation and British Computers (Allen and Unwin)

The Alternative Government (Trentham)

The Violent Society (Cass).

Learning to live in the Violent Society (Author-house)

Contributor Which Way (Joseph)

A Radical Future (Cape)

Contributor to the Times, the New York Times, Sunday Times.

ACKNOWLEDGEMENTS

And thanks to Natasha for her sub-editing from distant Austin, Texas to Leonora for her diligent typing and to Gillian, Josh and Daniel for 'being there'.

JOURNEYS

BERDICHEV TO BASILDON

I have often thought how my life would have been if I had started off in Basildon and ended up in Berdichev. Put it down to the sliding door of your life – events happen differently to what you prepare for - well described in a 1998 film by Peter Howitt.

The simple fact is that I got stuck in the advice business and I am still in there. It is something to be an MP with the largest constituency in the country but it is quite another to have to keep an eye on the Jewish community which has kept me up all night and I have never fully recovered.

Many of the quirks of life can be explained by being in the right place and at the right time (in Yiddish, there is also a long standing attempt to explain the events which you cannot predict but happen anyway. It's 'beshert' – then there is the nice warning sign for those who look too closely into the future, 'man tracht' and got lacht' (in English it may not have the same cutting edge, man plans and G-d laughs).

Why start with Berdichev? My father, Borach, was born in the town in 1878. At one time it was the place for any religious or adventurous Jew to aspire to live. It was a remarkable place for Jews, to feel comfortable in their prayers and lifestyle. I am talking about a small city close to Odessa, a centre of Jewish energy, culture and awareness. 1832 is a good starting point in understanding its Jewish environment. According to a local census of 1732 with the permission of the lady of the domain Tereza (Theresa) Zawisha, the leader of the town, granted a charter to the Jewish Guild of Taylors freeing them from interference by the communal authorities (kahal). The Jewish population gradually increased so that, according to the 1765 census the Jews numbered 1220 out of the total population of 1541. There were some outstanding scholars at the time, including Rav Levi Yitzchak of Berdichev. (1740-1810). Chassidic Tzaddick and Rebbe. He was a favourite personality of the third generation of the Chassidic movement. Others that came later included Lieber "the great", Joseph "the Harif" and "The Zaddick", Levi Isaac of Berdichev, the author of "Kedushat Levi".

Another influence event occurred in 1797 when Prince Radziwill granted seven Jewish cloth merchants the monopoly of the cloth trade in Berdichev and in the first half of the 19th Century the town's commerce was concentrated in Jewish hands. Jews founded scores of trading companies and banking establishments.

When the pre-marriage contract was written for Rabbi Levi Yitzchak of Berdichev's niece, he told them to write: "The wedding will take place, G-d willing, with good mazel, in the holy city of Jerusalem and if, G-d forbid, Moshiach ('Messiah') has not arrived by then, the wedding will take place in Berdichev". The sliding door in action.

The city began to prosper, albeit slowly, and the Jewish numbers increased to become the second largest Jewish community in Russia to close on 40,000, but anti-Semitic acts increased and so there was a movement away to the West. Life was tough for the Jews as their funds were reduced by the authorities, hitting education and general welfare. According to the 1897 census only 58 percent of Jewish males and 32 percent of Jewish females were able to read or write any language, for the vast majority of Jews at this time were without any occupation.

In the first years of the new century, Borach Moonman, like many other Jews, was called to the army and with little or no training were immediately thrust into front line action in the bitter war with Japan. The final outcome of the conflict drifted on with no clear signal to the serving men. Borach with his immediate colleagues took the decision to return home seeing that there was no pay and little food. It was here that Borach made the crucial decision to say farewell to his family and head west – no easy decision given the thousands of miles with meagre funds and little documentation to make for a port which would take him to the United States or England. In the following weeks close to the German coast, he waited to join up with his three sisters who were in some distress in Berdichev as the Russians had closed the synagogues and effectively ended communal life in the town. The sisters were sure that they would make it to the States but decided to go along with Borach. However such was the chaos in the embarkation process that they were separated and he made the journey alone, while they landed in New York he arrived and settled in the city of Liverpool.

One final word about Jewish Berdichev. Representative of the typical Jewish shtetl (community); It was compact, inward looking and everyone knew their role and the role of others. It had eighty synagogues and its Ministers were celebrated and known throughout the Ukraine. It was the model used in the writings for Shalom Aleichem and Mendole Mokber Seforim. Alas, in the early 1919 the Jews were victims of a systematic massacre (pogrom) organised by the government, an omen of an even greater tragedy when the Nazis took control in October 5, 1941. They established an extermination unit in the city and all Jews were murdered. Years later hankering to return to the 'city of Rabbis', often called the Jerusalem of Volhynia, yet again Jews re-established life there and naturally set up a synagogue.

LIVERPOOL

The Moonmans were in milk. With few opportunities in this bustling seaport for a foreigner, however keen Borach might be to find work, perhaps it was no surprise that he turned to what he knew best, the milk business. He set up a small delivery chain with mainly Jewish customers and also helped initially with the cows based a mile or so away. There was not a great deal of opportunity to improve his financial situation unlike some other immigrants who early on bought the odd run down houses and improved their status. But Borach was content to be away from the threat of pogroms and because of his optimistic attitude and he was welcomed by his customers in all weathers. Perhaps over the years he was a little too absent minded in collecting the bills of his needy customers or if they told him that they were down on their luck. He was soon helped by another immigrant, Leah Bernstein, who had travelled from Lithuania with her sister. Once married they helped each other to learn the new language, the new culture and also to jointly run the milk business. Borach was proud that he never missed a day's deliveries while pushing a heavy wooden dandy. Further help was on its way as every eighteen months the family increased in size which meant more hands for the deliveries (and more mouths to feed).

By the time I arrived after eight girls, there was much excitement. I was given a small but prestigious delivery round including the nearby massive Sacred Heart Church in Kensington. The nuns were very kind to me, delighted too that after the long the spell of Borach's girls now there was a boy. I enjoyed biscuits with them only interrupted by school time or the church bells drawing my attention to the powerful statue of the Christ figure. My parents always liked me to hurry back but I did enjoy my daily visit to Sacred Heart. "Why come to Liverpool?" Some customers would ask my mother. She would re-tell her story – often told by other immigrants who had had the same experience. They had paid the ship's captain a price to go to New York but travelling via Liverpool, he would announce "we are here". The corrupt captain would clear his ship. "Look around" he said. "Look at those buildings - a great city" but Leah was happy despite her mistake and her ignorance as it had brought her to the city where she met and married Borach – a fate changing moment indeed.

Watching life as youngsters we lived a third of our waking life on the streets. The current dangers whereby parents accompany children to school were not an issue. In the evenings "around Prescot Street" and Paddington life was like a large community hall - a ground not only for young Jewish boys and girls but also for non-Jews... until you were called in or screamed at ... "eisen time.." (eat now!)

Who else was on the street? The Missionaries. They did not have fancy names like the current "Jews for Jesus" campaign. They were regarded as a joke as they paraded through the streets around Paddington. As children we followed them and – encouraged by our parents – we derided and sang rather dubious Yiddish songs about them but it was friendly enough and as evening approached the Missionaries would talk to the older boys about Liverpool life rather than Christ's message.

The Protestant Orange Lodge members were also on the streets. They were lively and noisy as they marched around the time of the anniversary of the Battle of the Boyne. From Everton down Moss Street to London Road they made a cheerful sound to wake everyone up (some complained they in fact had been forced from their beds).

There was a less welcome element on the streets who were those looking for a fight. For me it meant a careful walk or play away from their cat calls. You were told to "Go back to Palestine". At the time I was five or six years of age and it didn't quite register with me or my friends. One day a friend said to me that Palestine was somewhere in the northern part of Liverpool so you would not have far to go.

Back in 1914 as the war with Germany approached, my father, like other immigrants, was not eligible for serving in the army but was drafted into what was called essential services, in his case the Liverpool Docks. The Moonman milk still flowed with my mother Leah and her young daughters all now at work.

Whilst normality of sorts was resumed after the war Borach returned and was determined to add to his previous round of deliveries. His wooden "dandy" was a heavy task as twice a day he travelled the streets the first round being as early as 6.30 am. He did not need to announce his arrival with a bell, popular in those days of street tradesmen, but he had a good voice and was regarded by the Jewish community as "Tevya the milkman".

Like so many men, my father could not explain why he put so much effort into his work but he did. He had to be an early riser for the milk would be placed outside the shop a little after 5am. I was amazed that anyone could possibly get up so early in the bleak winter and expose himself to the cold. How awful! Ma would complain that he should "hang the milk and look after yourself" (this was said when he had a chill or pain, which was not often). To this he would merely grunt a reply, if pressed, he would remind us of his responsibility to his wife and to his family. His pleasures were few; not for him the drinking and gambling which were so much in evidence in Liverpool 7 instead he played dominoes. "Dominoes is a game for ordinary men, cards for the wealthy and chess for the intellectuals" he would say to the other players, whilst the dominoes were brought out of a highly decorative Crawford's biscuit tin. Never once did he play in our house. Perhaps my mother thought it was too much like gambling. Just as my father would not express his reasons for working so energetically, ma could not explain her intense likes and dislikes. Dominoes might be an OK game which she would even take part in if encouraged by her friends. However, should a row take place between her and my father she would use the domino game as an irritant.

What about Ma? She was the essential source from which many of my sisters' ideas flourished. She was patient and although she had little knowledge of English, a wider range of gestures and Yiddish became well known and meaningful in the district and in the milk shop.

I loved the cinema. I was devoted to "the moving pictures" (as a mate called the shows) from the time I was 6 or 7. Not quite like Philip French, the outstanding film critic. He got the bug when he was four.

By the time I was 8, I already knew the difference in a film's ratings. An "A" certificate (meant under 16s had to be accompanied by an adult, preferably family, but every afternoon you could hear several kids asking any passing adult "can you take me in mister?" Then once inside you ran to the other end of the cinema. The "U" certificate got you in without trouble but I would swap the action films for the cartoons and fairy tales of "U" certificate any day.

My parents were less keen on my cinema-going and arranged that I spend any spare time in a choir – so I was duly enrolled in Princes Road Synagogue. It was a novelty to be able to blast off your voice and climb the ancient, often dangerous staircase up to the choir loft. It was fun and friendly and I found a mate in Ron and we were paid six pence a month. It all came to a head when I discovered that another boy with no greater voice sang an extra part and being paid three times as much as Ron and me. 'He' being Frankie Vaughan. I tackled the choirmaster about the pay difference and he said he had promised Frankie's mother and could not alter it. After a few more rows my friend Ron and I quit – it was my first industrial dispute. I thought we might chance a strike but I could not rely on the other 'old fogies'. Later on Frankie even took my one singing claim to fame: "Give me the moonlight". I also met him when I was an MP and we spoke about the choir days. He offered an apology about "being on the higher pay rate". Mind you, we laughed it all off except when I said "what about the song I lost – give me the moonlight!"

Liverpool's Brownlow Hill environment covered a small part of the inner city but it was packed with culture and activity.

I have no wish after all this time to re-open the issues as to who provided the best 'cheder' in Liverpool as the case was strongly made for the "Talmud

Torah" (religious tuition); but for the select few who attended Mr Sprince in Elizabeth Street we have no doubt the venerable gentleman had the edge. He offered an early example of private education and he encouraged pupils, one at a time, to read, read and read. Mrs Sprince would sit nearby consuming large amounts of schmaltz herrings, ever watchful and offering the boys a biscuit whenever our behaviour justified reward.

Payment for lessons was another matter and was arranged by a goods transaction so my father Borach provided the milk and Sprince the tuition. I have to add that the butcher Bredski was also a part of the transactions but that is another story.

The Albert shop of breads and cakes (opposite Crown Street Synagogue) was controlled by the Albert women, formidable, and to a small boy, quite fearsome.

I hardly imagined that one day I would marry into the family. Walking the street today, as I approached Abercromby Square for the university, I am overwhelmed with the past and the lifestyle of the tight-knit community at the time which existed around Paddington, Prescot Street, Kensington and Islington.

In the thirties with more children to help and add to the milk deliveries with a growing number of customers there was a family confidence. But again fate intervened quite dramatically. The business came to a stop on Saturday December 20th 1940.

THE BLITZ

A new war and even more tragedy hit the families of Britain, including a continuous Nazi bombing of Liverpool.

The centre of Liverpool took a heavy pounding. The seaport was an essential hub of movement with all manner of supplies to and from the ships, particularly those from the United States. Hardly a day passed with any quiet. On this particular December night in 1940 a landmine dropped within a few hundred yards from our home which brought everything down in its wake. Rescuers dug us all out of the cellar and my mother sustained some injuries but fortunately they were not too serious.

Previously, the children of my age in the area were evacuated to North Wales but I chose to stay in the city with Sylvia, my next sister who was closest in age to me, that night when we lost the business and our home.

Still, the bombing for us was all a close run thing of survival. On this occasion Sylvia and I always slept in the top floor of the house and we would certainly have been in our beds on a normal night as it was close to midnight. But on this occasion, as Chanukah/Christmas approached, all the family were home for the festivities so we were on the ground floor close to the basement level listening to their gossip and their tales of all their travels! ("Beshert").

When after some hours we all surfaced on to the street with fire engines and wardens, police and pipes everywhere, the scene was lit up like a film set. We were all taken into a nearby council building to rest the remainder of the night. In the morning an official interviewed all the families to check whether we had family elsewhere to stay or if we needed to be "evacuated" out of the city. Fortunately we had a sister in Southport, twenty miles away, so my parents chose to go to her. That night and the following morning was tough, recognising the terrible sense of loss and upheaval. We were so close to death and then we realised that the destruction of our home meant the end of the milk business after all these years for which my father had toiled with such enthusiasm and love.

The Liverpool Echo reported in a review a while later "the terror and sadness revealed a sense of unity, the best of the human spirit, countless acts of self-sacrifice, courage and kindness. Those in distress and great need found help from neighbours who cleared the rubble, provided sandwiches and tea, plus shelter and longer-term re-housing. The aid agencies also acted quickly. Three people over 80 years of age, found in the wreckage of their homes were re-housed the same day in Shropshire.

Lancashire miners arrived with picks and shovels to dig in the wreckage of homes. Two soldiers dragged a piano out of a bombed store and began playing "There'll Always Be An England".

In Southport my sister's flat was quite small. It was a struggle but we all managed. We had travelled lightly with hardly any luggage. There were so many of us in one room that it soon became obvious that we had to search for some other arrangements but to me it was all very confusing.

Southport, a quiet seaside resort, was to be my home for the years ahead. It was so very different to the noise and experience for a boy looking for adventures in the big city.

My father, finding himself suddenly retired from his business kept his spirits up, as far as I could tell, by regular daily visits to the synagogue in Arnside Road. He had always been a regular attender back home whether in Berdichev or Liverpool's Crown and Russell Street's synagogues. My mother managed as best as she could in the limited space of a flat and my sisters took any available job. Ironically one sister, Eve, worked in a wartime 'deferred occupation' consisting of running a milk round – automatic vehicle and all.

I had to start again in a new school and, as there were no immediate vacancies in the existing school buildings, I was placed in a church school which was filled with evacuees from Bootle. The evacuees were tough and cynical because they had left their families behind yet here we were only a 15 mile distance away from their homes.

I certainly learned a few tricks in survival. The school was in difficulties because only two teachers had come with the hundred or so pupils and so discipline was non-existent. Timetables could not operate so there were delayed starting times and inevitably there were early closing times. Not surprisingly, the quiet folk of the district made sure the police were always close by throughout the day. The atmosphere, I recall, was full of conflict and anger so my parents with the help of a sister, paid for me to go to a private school and again another massive switch for an 11 year old.

Now I was at Croxton. I was hardly the ideal candidate for the snooty atmosphere, particularly as it was "preparatory" and I could never grasp exactly what it was preparing us for. I was much older than most boys but it did not matter because only two things were vital. Mornings were taken up largely with Latin and the afternoons were on the field playing football. Listening to Latin was like a dream for me and fortunately the teacher was so in love with the subject he never bothered to call on me or question my knowledge although one boy did say to me: he must think you know it all – where did you learn it?

On reflection I suspect that the teacher was hardly aware I was in the classroom but the afternoon soccer was great and because of my size it was not long before I captained the side and scored goals all afternoon.

However, even at this school I did not last long as the family realised they were unable to keep up the fees. Fortunately a vacancy opened up at the town's regular school, Christ Church.

So I was not long at Croxton the posh preparatory school. One of life's little jokes - and curiously some 25 years later when the school hit on bad times and the head was dismissed for serious allegations of sexual child abuse with the boys it looked as if they might close so they began a fund raising event and they asked me to front an appeal for funds!

At 13 I almost failed to have my barmitzvah which is an important event in the life and learning of a young Jewish boy. On the Day of Atonement when all the congregants were fasting, for a 'dare' I threw, some messy cream cakes from the top of the women's gallery which hit the 'important' women in the synagogue. There were calls for my exclusion and expulsion. Some of the elders blamed my poor old dad, saying he couldn't handle his 'wayward son'. Fortunately, the Rabbi valued my father and said the barmitzvah would proceed. A punishment was offered by a senior lady whose hat was affected and must have seen 'something in me, (she said) as she would meet with me once a week for a while to discuss Torah and Responsibility. I soon appreciated her advice and kind interest (plus biscuits and tea). We became close friends.

As far as the war was concerned, I was aware that people around me reacted with cheer to good news but as families were split up when a father or son had to go in the army or when there was news of a fatality or injury it suddenly all went flat and a different mood prevailed.

I had absolutely no interest in school or the teachings. However at Christ Church I was fortunate to have discovered a teacher, Mrs Quirk, who recognised that I might have "a future" in contrast to most teachers I had known who doubted I had any ability whatsoever. She spoke to me in a friendly way and encouraged me to edit the school magazine which I produced weekly – all handwritten, it was a terrific feeling and got other boys wanting me to publish their stories, their ideas and gossip. Funnily enough my grades in other subjects also improved.

However at Christmas 1943, still not yet 14, I felt I really would like to leave school and get a job and as an opening occurred the family agreed for me to try for an interview. I got the job but we had to appeal to the local labour exchange that I be allowed to take employment before the normal school leaving age. I won't forget what the manager of the exchange said when I approached him "technically you cannot leave so young but these are difficult times with the war and we must all do our bit, permission granted." I did not realise that I was working for the war effort! Working at 13 was enormously helpful in my later political life. Many Labour politicians would go on and on about being a product of the "factory floor at 14 or 15" so I would confront and impress an audience with my proud claim "13 years and on the job".

EARLY JOBS

What did I want to do? To write, to set things up, play around with ideas which I was able to do when writing and editing the school magazine so my first job was an assistant in the small newspaper office of the local regional paper the Liverpool Echo. This meant mainly travelling round to the street sellers and stamping the latest news in the stop press section of the paper. Usually I had to do this on my knees on the early printed copy but the sellers were friendly and delighted to get updated news, racing results and they could shout "latest edition" in the afternoon all due to my stencil in the stop press column! The sellers invited me to sell copies at the railway station for the Empire News late on Saturday nights providing the latest soccer results. I enjoyed both jobs and I was stimulated by the branch manager of the newspaper who would talk politics from the moment I came in the morning until late "going home time". He gave out a strong left-wing message even whilst we shared a sandwich. After a year or more a regular job came up with a firm of printers which would offer an apprenticeship in the trade which my father strongly advised me to take. I agreed. I suppose my reasoning was that printing was linked to journalism which I still wanted to learn and my father was keen for me, like many others of his generation who believed an apprenticeship was a safety net to have in the future. It was a small firm with two partners dealing with general jobbing work and also the printing of one weekly publication, Pugh's Property Journal, on the various sales and investment opportunities in Merseyside and North Wales. It also meant travelling daily to Liverpool, involving a short rail journey. The first two years were interesting but then into my third year I wondered how far I could carry on as the apprenticeship was an extraordinary seven years. Other young apprentices I met in the trade believed it was intended to provide extra years of cheap labour for the bosses and I was convinced they were right so my thoughts and energy started to drift elsewhere whilst aiming to serve out my apprenticeship – but seven years!

I was becoming interested in the ways of making use of the rest of the hours of the week although six and a half days each week in the print did not leave much scope. Still there was one Saturday morning off in two and I found in the Labour Party (in this very Tory seat of Southport), a group of like-minded Labourites who would come together and take part in discussions. To put it mildly I was out of my depth but so was another youngster Michael English who was later to become an MP for a Nottingham seat. However I was learning fairly fast and helped by attendance at the YMCA where a weekly debate took place on a wide range of subjects every Thursday night which stimulated my interest and my time. I realised I had needed to grapple with a variety of subjects for the debates and so my search for knowledge began. I did not know this at the time - how could I – but then I have been on a learning curve all my life.

I still wanted to make use of the other evenings in the week. I applied to take an economics course at the Liverpool College of Commerce (after work on Tuesday) which prompted a strange, possibly hilarious admissions interview when the course lecturer asked "what are your qualifications?" I replied none; he tried other questions and again I had to say "none". He was Campbell Frazer and he said "we need you – you can attend classes – but you will not be able to sit the exams, but come in, we start tonight". He was a man of great understanding who later became the Chief Executive of Dunlop.

I welcomed the offer and also the help and support of many others, including Richard Stokes who was then at the Cotton Commission and who became a real friend – and still is to this day.

The ad hoc education and support encouraged me to share ideas with other young apprentices in printing in Liverpool and beyond so we decided to set up the first Guild of Young Printers under the sponsorship of our Union, the Typographical Association. The local Chief Executive of the TA Owen

Ellis was delighted that I had begun to involve all youngsters in the trade and we were soon questioning policy at the main union meetings.

My apprenticeship years continued as my busy round of Labour and trade union meetings economic classes increased. As soon as one "academic" session finished I signed up for an Extra Mural Course at Liverpool University in Public Speaking. I also wanted to know how to say what I knew! The first time I went to the class was a shock. I was late and the class were on the first exercise – to stick your tongue out for two minutes. (The mouth exercise). To see a handful of people all standing with their tongues out and looking so solemn. It was a riot. Later, the lecturer explained it would cause our mouths to relax. Yet my first reaction of laughing out loud continued quietly for almost half the session.

I very much needed the tips and support of the public speaking course if I wanted to be confident at the YMCA debating society and with friends like Richard Stokes I needed to get my words together.

In the third year of my apprenticeship I did take a break as I was entitled to a week's holiday I went with a couple of friends who also worked in print to the Isle of Man. From Liverpool this was a popular and cheap way of going "abroad". The small island meant a four hour boat trip from Liverpool with many passengers invariably heading for the toilets with frequent rough seas but the moment we landed the sun appeared and did not leave us for the entire week. We stayed at the men and boys camp, the Cunningham. The main feature was a weekly party night when the girls of the village (and other tourists) were allowed in and that meant a lively and somewhat crazy time. The other activity of the week was the long standing football "international" between the Scottish and the English residents. It was taken most seriously by everyone inside and outside the summer camp and for some reason I made it to the English XI but even more surprisingly whilst waiting for kick off the coach at the camp put a band across my chest and said "you are the captain today!"

At this point, it must be said that at the age of seven I was told I had to wear glasses and I would be able to discard them at 12. In fact I am still wearing them today. In the game there was much heavy tackling, much noise from the two sets of players and supporters but no goals and one did not seem likely. However fate intervened and in the last few minutes England were awarded a free kick from 30 yards from the opponents' goal. All of a sudden all my team ran to the opposite goal including me until I was told "go back and take it". There was no way could I see the goal but I was now alone with the muddy ball. I looked around with my dim eyesight. Time was slipping by but I could not see anyone. I heard the referee in the distance shouting with increasing volume, "get on with the bloody ball" so I hit the ball with all my might in the direction of the referee and in the gloom then there was pandemonium as all the players in front of me were screaming with frantic delight. Apparently my shot had hit on the crossbar and then a team mate forced it in the net. Game over and my kick ensured that I did not pay for a single round of drinks that night but I had to tolerate being called "captain" all night by the team and the visiting girls.

The next year my weeks holiday could not have been more different. With my friend Dennis, another printer, we had received trade union scholarships to attend an economic and political conference for trade unionists at the International Labour Office (ILO) in Geneva. It was my first time abroad. The agenda was pretty full and that was how I personally wanted it. Dennis was less enthusiastic about the content but still enjoyed the contrast with every day work.

As I approached my 21st birthday my apprenticeship was coming to an end. Although the seventh year had not been reached I was now faced with the choice of conscription to the Army, Navy or Air Force.

I preferred the Air Force and Dennis assured me that "you never get your first choice" so at his conscription interview he had chosen the Army and ended up in the Air Force which was what he preferred. Armed with such insider information I did likewise. I volunteered for the Infantry and ended up in the Infantry - the Liverpool Kings Regiment to be precise. Dennis tried to console me. "It doesn't work every time".

I still had a little time before the actual call up and as I had an interest in all forms of music I helped to set up a jazz club at the Temperance Institute in Southport with a number of really great local musicians including a fine clarinettist Eric Lister and the Roscoe brothers who were exceptional. It became a lively weekly event called "Mooneys" (my jazz title!) I also had a pseudonym Elya for a music column I wrote for the local Southport newspaper. This highlighted future musical events in the town and the appearance of the swinging Les Douglas Band. Elya is my Hebrew name incidentally.

In union matters I was nominated by the Typographical Society to attend the Labour Party Conference but I just missed out in the ballot, beaten by Joe Wade who later became the Union General Secretary. The branch was not too upset as they told me it was important to get your name forward.

My Trade Union Officer attempting to reassure me said, "you'll be fine, you are a late developer". He meant well but in fact everything I had done or was doing was the opposite. He roared with laughter when I told him at seven I was reproducing posters for our outside lavatory door. At 8, I extended the design, with reports on what our neighbours were up to, even giving them ratings on their friendliness and their attitude to our family, but at 13 I was writing the whole magazine for my school at Christ Church attributing the juicy bits to anonymous boys.

Not much to say about conscription except to note I did the infantry square bashing at Chester, made some friends, and I was offered the incentive to volunteer for a further six months (above the two year limit) and the catch was to attend a 12 month Russian course at Cambridge University. I never did discover whether this was a crash course in spying. In the end the offer never materialised.

I travelled to several army commands and somehow my documents must have carried a description that I was keen on education. Hence as soon as I arrived at a base I was sent on an educational course of varying description, often having to travel a distance to the college concerned. I was given a ration allowance for the journey which usually consisted of a tin of beans and as one sergeant in catering said "just take this to a nearby café and they will heat it and open it for you. There is a lot of good will about". I never put that to the test as I bought a tin opener. One curious thing happened before I completed my army service. In Southport there was a shortage of Labour candidates and because I was based fairly close to the town my old colleagues wanted me to stand. "Do not worry" said a close friend and Labour fixer – "you will not win the local seat but just allow us to put your name forward". The temptation to stand for Labour was such that I did allow my name to go forward and of course it was a hopeless seat for Labour, Park Ward. The agent saw to all the essential details and there were no meetings to address except that the Tories got wind of the fact that I was an "army man" (I do not think they realised I was still in the army) so they completely ignored me and the campaign in the ward. In the end I did comparatively well and avoided what would have been a highly complicated success!

Having acquired all this knowledge and learning through the extra mural department and the College of Commerce in Liverpool I decided not to return to the print industry but to try for a place at the University of Liverpool. One of the lecturers I had met, Tom Lupton, gave me much advice and support in my application and yet on the day prior to sitting for the examination, my father died which left me emotionally stranded. When I did get around to thinking of my chances on the full time course I thought that I had lost it but a week later Tom Lupton said "if you are still interested we can provide you with a sitting under an invigilator". It was a boon that I took advantage of and duly found myself in the Diploma course in Social Studies.

After chasing all the scraps of knowledge and reading by myself the feeling that I was no longer on my own but part of a group of students with a common interest to study was fantastic. Not that they were as time limited as I was but the group spent a lot of time together and I suppose I was in the middle of the age range with a couple of youngsters and some elderly men and women but I coped. Essays were novel, discussions I enjoyed but initially I held back as I wanted to settle in with the way ideas and news were related. Also in class there was also a discipline, not previously encountered, when the tutor was Head of the Department the redoubtable

Professor Tom Simey. It was hard work but considering where I had come from I had time – at least more time to plan for whatever I wanted to do.

I shared a flat near to the University with a biochemistry student, Roy Levin, who I discovered, had the same off beat sense of humour as I had although I was ten years older. We edited together the annual Student rag magazine, Panto sphinx which produced an article of sexy ladies and the pictures I used were from my family's stock file. Unfortunately relatives of one sexy female (from the 20s) were strictly unhappy. Roy and I had to eat humble pie over two meals with all the lady's cousins. Fortunately all the participants, as we were, were Jewish. "That makes it worse" screamed one relative, "that is my Auntie Sarah you two mishugines (madmen) have abused"......

I had managed to get fair results at the university and so I looked around for a job. It was not so easy. Roy, however, went on to great things as a Professor in Sheffield. I had hoped to stay around Merseyside in the North but nothing materialised so I made for London.

Bessie Braddock the redoubtable Liverpool MP gave me advice on getting on a council "we need people like you" and with another stalwart in the city Lady Margaret Simey, wife of my college professor Tom Simey set me up for a ward selection conference in Abercromby. I was introduced to a number of ward members and they seem to like what I offered, "we need youth" I was told.

It all seemed a foregone conclusion that I would start on the political ladder here in the city of my birth - that is until the night of selection. The hall was quite small and there were no more than a dozen people, many known to me when five minutes after the starting time twenty or more men, women and children (plus a couple of cats) I spoke quite briefly to the meeting but my opponent did not speak at all. As the counted vote was taken to represent the ward the "late" comers nominated and all voted in unison for one of their numbers. I was hardly in the ballot but now I was out! Later Margaret Simey comforted me by saying "I am afraid that the RC (Catholic) family decided to take over", once again highlighting the crude, cynical nature of Liverpool politics where a Protestant party existed for many years.

IN LONDON

I chose three ways to meet my "box of interest" and lifestyle. I became a resident of Toynbee Hall, a well-regarded University settlement in the East where Jimmy Mallon and Clem Attlee made their mark in social welfare. As a resident you were expected to assist in a broad range of the social services in the evenings and weekends irrespective of how you earned a living during the day. Hence several senior business managers and the head of the Post Office were treated in the same way. I elected to start with mentoring some young men and all help out with the legal aid service which was manned by several volunteer solicitors.

So much for social interests but my full time job was something else. Although I had no wish to return to printing but the offer from Daily Mirror Newspapers operating in London and in Manchester was certainly attractive. They were keen to recruit me as I had the combined experience of print and a university qualification. The job was hardly demanding; as a problem chaser to assess the number of incidents or mishaps during the run of the daily edition. I gained some good insights of top brass thinking but it did not hold me for long. I did learn one thing – always give the public what they want. The case in point: circulation was slipping and from on high we were told get the "slippage" approach.

The result of the change? On the day's front page appeared a sad looking hound, Scruffy by name who was to die by 4pm unless an owner came to his rescue and who would provide a home? They came in their droves. The queues formed early and continued until noon and cries of "we want Scruffy" could be heard well down Deansgate. The caring newspaper responded magnificently with its good intentions and I was dispatched to every dog's home within a thirty mile radius to get as many dogs as we could muster so Scruffy (and his look-a like) could be saved. They were all saved and so was circulation of this tabloid newspaper. Inexplicably the figures started to rise as a trickle until the trend was up and by month end we were clearly and firmly going well. There was a smile on everyone's faces – management and print workers. One foreman said to me who did not know too much about my role in the escapade "the old man would not allow anything terrible to happen to this pathetic looking animal. The story was picked up in many parts of the world's media.

The fact that we offered a goodly number of dogs who hardly resembled Scruffy did not seem to matter because they all had the same desperate, anxious look and appearance.

After a while I was fortunate to take up a post in London at the British Institute of Management in the area dealing with personnel, incentive schemes and communications. I certainly had to learn on the job!

In the meantime I started to attend Labour party meetings in Stepney.

Before settling into my London life with much increased action, I accepted a call to help as a volunteer with the major earthquake in Greece in the summer of 1953.

It arose when I heard a radio programme in which Prince Philip called for young able bodied people to help with and lend support following the Greek earthquakes in Cephalonia. I decided this seemed a valuable way to help as the pictures and requests on television were dramatic and troubling. I flew out to Athens and that was the easy bit but from then on I had to pick up a boat which meant waiting for one that was a medium sized craft to enter the shattered port of Cephalonia. The ship would stop some way off shore whilst we passengers were off loaded into tiny crafts only larger than a recovery boat. With the water fairly buoyant this was a trial and test for anyone's constitution and enthusiasm. I shared the boat with a small family and as the mother was in a frightful way she just loaded me with her baby which had a good effect on my troubled stomach as I now had a job to take my mind off the journey. After this trial I had to wait for a vehicle to take us to the high point of the Island where all the volunteers were bussed. If the still small boat was one trial here was another as we all crammed into the small truck.

The journey by truck consisted of climbing the many hills and then more hills. You could not see where you were except when you lifted the rear tarpaulin cover – after one peep I decided it was best not to know about the mountain climb! Then I was dropped off with no-one else and with a map, a case and the blazing sun. More climbing for an hour and then to be greeted by the young men and women. After that journey I could take on anything. There was much friendship and interest in each other as the volunteers had responded from many countries.

Apart from the physical demands of our work, many of the domestic problems were due to a lack of supplies from the aid authorities and so improvisation in eating and resting was necessary. We made tea with the flowers which had survived the turmoil and we rested when the sun was most hostile.

Having lived through the blitz and some unsettled housing I enjoyed the challenge of the physical work and I was chosen as one of the team leaders. The reward? The name of "Mr Fixit" along with two others from the Scandinavian countries. To honour the occasion, despite the intense heat, we had a delightful ceremony over a box of biscuits the gift of a new arrival (half a biscuit each) – for team leaders!

It was a tough assignment but our daily routine was to be up and out by 6am and to return by midday to avoid the heat and the out again later. The work was basic – road building, removing the pathways of the cracked and heavily flung rubble from the earthquake. The task was enormous but I had to keep up the heavy physical side as I was "partnered" with a young Belgian girl who was most adept and controlled in all she did.

Several times at night we heard rumblings and vibrations which caused us to awake and to be ready should further earthquakes occur and to be alert and get dressed.

LOCAL POLITICIANS AND TOYNBEE HALL

I was in Spitalfields and actively working in my spare time with the Labour Party and soon showing interest and helping with the various activities and I was elected as a Labour Councillor. It was like no other local Labour party I have ever encountered (although I was assured there were many other parties with little political discussion and yet, real comradeship). The constituency and the ward included Petticoat Lane and the ward officers and the culture was all "market". Any reference to budgets was invariably about the cost of trades stalls. What can be achieved by the traders in this way in the space of half an hour was astonishing. At the close of the meeting everyone was in a cheerful state with "deals done" so we retired to one of the market trader's homes for a large supper which seemed to have been prepared hours ago. As a single man with a limited budget I ate well.

The Irish pub do on the occasional Saturday night was pure booze. I was accepted by the party leadership, I suppose because I had no axe or stall. I led the Stepney Council in advance of the change in the larger borough of Tower Hamlets.

At the British Institute of Management and even in Toynbee Hall I was intrigued in the way effective management could be a focal point for an individual's purpose and development. Having initiated a programme of lectures under the heading of the manager and the organisation with much reference to an individual's skills I started my first book on this theme. I am told there is nothing like the excitement of seeing your first writing in book form published by an academic publisher. It received good reviews and it was a useful aid to the growing number of management skills courses such as at South West Technical College where I gave a course over the winter and spring.

It was all pressure as my work at the Institute was succeeding, I was the only left-wing voice so I was in demand to speak at conferences and seminars throughout the country. Unfortunately the Director, John Marsh, quite a radical himself, felt I had, as he put it, "gone a little too far for the Institute as I understand you want to be a Labour parliamentary candidate. If you accept this it will be your decision but the Institute would prefer you sought other avenues of work". Looking back it was a bit crushing coming from someone I had admired for his radical views. I left to fight the strong Tory seat of Chigwell and Ongar against John Biggs Davison. People often say why fight and spend your time in such a hopeless seat and I know many candidates are impatient and will "hold out" for something better. I had no regrets as I learned a great deal in the demands and organisation of the larger constituency and not confined to one ward or borough. The seat was a mixture but largely laid back Tories and with a few small patches of Labour and here the locals were very warm and affectionate to me. I also developed a close respect and regard for my opponent indeed when I did eventually become and MP – he and I were 'pairs'. That is, we arranged via the Parliamentary whips to be paired for non-attendance at important votes when other commitments prevented us from being at Westminster.

So politics were now centre stage for me between my local council work and performing as a prospective parliamentary candidate but now away from the BIM I had to see what I could do given that in 1961 we were certainly several years away from an election which clearly meant that I had to get on with the business of earning a living. .

The outlet I chose was an academic one. I returned to the North West as a research fellow at the University of Manchester. It was to examine and report on the changing patterns of organisations and what it could mean to the individual. It was an interesting addition to my book and my years at BIM. Mainly it was a chance to study under a very clever expert in the field, Professor Reg Revans. This meant another geographical move to Manchester whilst my young family stayed in London but it was not an easy option as the research meant visiting a number of mills in Lancashire and racing back to attend Council meetings in London as well as looking after my "seat" (however hopeless) at weekends.

Each of these tasks produced important steps in my personal development and learning process. First, the research at UMIST was immediate and likely to involve action research enabling me to undertake personal visits over a wide area and it resulted in another book. "Communication in an Expanding Organisation".

As a result I got my MSc and the second "reward" for my crazy years in the early sixties was that, although I was unsuccessful in Chigwell and Ongar, the seat it put me in the right frame for a better Labour constituency with the national and local parties so I was selected for the new town of Basildon which I fought in 1966 and became its MP.

It was an odd part of Essex as from a superficial appearance it would seem like it could be a solid Labour domain but the "new towners" those new to this part of Essex still had their loyalties, families and interests to the original areas they had left of Bethnal Green and Dagenham and were not immediately interested in Basildon. I encountered the phrase many times over, 'let the Essex lot get on with it' and of course it would change in time as they too would be the "Essex lot".

But I was "in" where I wanted to be ever since I became active in the young printers and had joined the Labour Party. I believed I could make a difference to the way life was lived and my knowledge of working class life could be of value to the Labour Party as I read that there was concern that not enough craftsmen and those who represented the streets were seldom adopted. Certainly there were some toffs after the Basildon seat. It was a wonderful feeling, I was in!

Although I had not given an undertaking to live within the constituency nor was it far to Westminster, we moved in given the need to cover such a large electorate. It was in fact the largest in the country, at the time, stretching from Brentwood, Shenfield on the more Tory districts to Billericay and up the A127 to Wickford which demanded more attention from a labour spokesman. Basildon was something of an enigma. A New Town it was - and I was told many times it had been winnable for Labour but there was an underbelly of voters wishing to be considered upmarket and this was shown in the way the New Town residents would embellish their houses – new front doors constantly changing, then a better standard of wood as they upped the stakes on their neighbours; then the wide open garden areas which gave an attractive sweep to the various streets of the town. Some acquired partial wooden fencing, then full fencing. As I canvassed over the years I noticed that the house front may have started like typical council houses but they all acquired the paraphernalia mentioned here to say nothing of the growing flower arrangements. At any rate it was my business to win the hearts and minds of the constituency despite a strange warning from an old Labour supporter in the town, "you will never do enough to keep them happy!"

Bearing in mind that I now held a Parliamentary seat I felt I should sort myself out as so much of what I had done (or achieved) had happened so quickly. Sometimes your experiences could be directed and even misdirected. What did I want to achieve? It may seem strange that I should only now be asking that of myself, particularly after I had become the standard bearer for the government party in Basildon.

I managed to get away for a little while before parliament settled in and my family thought it was sensible to answer some of these questions away from all my jobs and commitments.

Why did I feel so comfortable and supportive in the Labour Party and its policies? Clearly it was not directly due to intense reading of the early pioneers although I respected the generations before me who must have considered similar questions. No, my socialist ideals were more fragmented but highly personal. My first chance to see what socialism represented and offered came from almost daily conversations with my first boss when I was 14 and working as a newsboy for the Liverpool Echo. He was an out and out communist and gave me the push to consider his ideas and reject the "selfish society". I learned a little to be able to share an argument a few years later with another person, my trade union officer in Liverpool, Owen

Ellis. Usually mild of manner he could be aroused if anyone in his presence ignored the Welsh contribution to society or if Labour's philosophies were challenged or ignored. He too had been in print all his life.

I learned so much, not only about the nature and demands of socialism and also why all in the working class had a responsibility to work for Labour to achieve power. Owen Ellis would always end up our meetings in the union printing office "we have no choice brother".

As I raced through my teens, the ideas of a fairer and just society became clearer to me. I was even able to join the other Labour supporters to make a noisy appearance at Tory meetings in the Cambridge Hall, Southport, when the visiting MP and Ministers spoke.

I was also reading and I became a regular at the local Southport library searching out Labour tracts.

When I did my national service in the infantry I never thought it odd whilst on guard duty to have a large tome "The Sparks of the Russian Revolution" alongside me – mind you the Duty Sergeant did show his concern!

Again looking back, at the Pier Head in Liverpool my union colleagues and I tried to start a Speaker's Corner I had read about the original one in London's Hyde Park. I used the technique devised by Ian Mikardo (the MP who became a good friend in later life); when there are no speakers areas or speakers bench you create one! All that happened was that a couple of us would start an argument and then another passer-by would stop and join in, and then another and another so that in less than fifteen minutes there was a full-blooded meeting and I moved around the circle and soon there were other debates and then one guy with a loud voice would call all to order. It became a real focal point and so the Labour case was heard amongst the scouse voices!

I also joined the Fabian Society but here the voices were more restrained and cautious. I had also attended a Fabian Summer School and the ideas were OK but I was indifferent to the social life which increasingly left me cold.

Throughout my early political years I found the organizational aspect of my work very satisfying, contacting speakers and making sure we had properly communicated with them. I found that my circle of union members and friends were only too willing to join me for marches, demos or debate. We were lively and a wee bit inspired

At the same time one or two well-meaning friends wondered whether my interest and growing commitment to the Labour movement might put a strain in my relationship with my father and family but this was not so. Dad was an engaging and liberal minded, thoroughly decent man and took immense satisfaction in what I was doing. I had found a voice and had the chutzpah to use it. He liked that. He was, like his family in Berdichev, hard working. He understood the need for an individual to work together with others of like mind.

As mother and father died whilst I was striving for political attention it forced me to work a little harder in all I was doing. I was also receiving attention and invitations to speak. I would often read the ideas of Jack London, Hillaire Belloc and George Bernard Shaw which helped to create and shape a wider reach to the main political theme of my speech which seemed to go down fairly well.

I had not read a great deal when compared to some of the people I was associating with – Balliol graduates and public schools and the like but I was catching up.

IN PARLIAMENT

At the time it seemed that parliament was in some ways the worst place to be if you were still on a learning curve. Little did I realise I would still be on a learning curve nearly fifty years later!

Knowledge of the House of Commons procedures and rituals were known by those who had been there some considerable time but generally the old stagers do not easily pass over their knowledge. It was, I suppose not a mean attitude but rather a sense of "you must learn for yourself". It was reflected by one older member to one of my fellow new entrants, Albert Booth (MP for Barrow), "we have spent some time learning the ropes, now we expect you to do the same". I shared a space in an alcove with Albert, a good solid shop floor worker and who, in time, rose to be a Cabinet Minister. Alas, illness robbed him of much of his working life but it did enable us to do a joint "Box and Cox" on the Middle East in visiting colleges. I naturally took the Israeli point of view and he argued the Arab case. There were differences between us but never unfairly expressed and never any recriminations in anger.

The Parliamentary Whips demanded regular attendance from new members in particular. This was not a hardship as I was only too keen to see how the House worked. You were put on a committee of a Bill that was going nowhere (and the Whips told you so but nevertheless expected your full attention and attendance at the proceedings). It also meant I discovered that if you did not know the subject, you would be unlikely to upset the applecart or the whips who simply wanted to get the bill through with the minimum of fuss and special pleading by a member.

The weeks passed quickly into months and I made two important decisions. First the Parliamentary Labour Party set up a number of panels and as I was already attending the Science and Technology Committee I was happy to agree to act as Chairman (there were no runners anyway!) and secondly I began to pursue my interests relating to Mental Health. In the 60s there was no select committee and the issues were somewhat unattractive and forgotten which caused me to push and persuade for the mentally ill and disabled across party lines. An informed committee of members might be possible.

Some friends outside the House offered help to provide backup and a secretariat was initiated outside the House. John Wilder, a terrific Chief Executive of the Psychiatric Rehabilitation Association (PRA) and Professor John Denham also a charismatic consultant at St Clements Hospital in the East End helped enormously. Our aim was to extract from Health Ministers details of the scale of the problem and hopefully to get the issue prioritised.

I personally raised the question and initiated debates on the floor of the House but the most successful device for this "pressure group" (coined by a Health Minister who was somewhat harassed in an argument) was the way we took over the Order Paper of Business with hundreds of written questions from every part of the House. It helped, I was aware, to raise the interest and status of mental health and it provoked at least one Health Minister having to consider where the next issue or campaign was coming from.

Science and Technology was less a campaign issue and the main focus of the committee was to plan and organise a monthly meeting with presentations from leaders in the field and the public agencies. Tony Benn as Minister for Technology during this parliament (1966-70) was a tremendous support to myself and to the group generally. He was one Minister who understood why and how it was necessary to keep the public aware of what the government was doing.

At this time, Patrick Gordon Walker had returned to the Cabinet after his difficulties at Smethwick. He was now the Labour MP for Leyton which he won in a by-election. He, in contrast to Tony Benn, was not comfortable with the "public interest and purpose" of our work. Harold

Wilson appointed him a Minister without Portfolio and that meant a very wide brief with significant oversight (not responsibilities) for Education and occasionally to heading up on Foreign Affairs. Clearly a complex brief. He approached me through the Whip's Office who expressed support in my acting as his aide (Parliamentary Private Secretary) and I saw this as a way of helping not only the PLP but also Patrick who, with his wife Audrey, were dear friends. Patrick was still rather shattered as a result of his experiences in the racist campaigns in Smethwick and where he lost his seat and much of his confidence.

I also kept a watchful eye on Patrick's PR image which was pretty low key. In attempting to get him a wider "Man" coverage it would be good for him to get known amongst the supporters and fan base of the local football team, Leyton Orient. I decided on a device, however corny deployed by Arthur Lewis, a former MP for covering the West Ham FC area – namely to get one of his agents to ring the ground on a match day and ensure, at half time a tannoy announcement that he return either to the front desk or to his constituency office. I know it worked with Arthur as he told me so. I decided to chance this device with Patrick who had practically no interest in soccer but he went along with it. I laid out the details and he assured me he would be at the ground. I duly made the call which was taken up at half time. "would the MP Patrick Gordon Walker return...." Unfortunately Patrick misjudged the timing of the game and was nowhere to be seen. That was the extent of my PR for him although I have been in a public place where such announcements have been made for the MP to leave immediately and I hope that he or she has bothered to show up!

At a Labour Party conference shortly afterwards, Tony Benn asked to see me and over his usual cup of tea (I wonder how he travelled with his favourite cup?) said that there was a vacancy to be his PPS. He continued that he was impressed with what I had achieved in the PLP's Technology Committee and would I take the job on? This was a complete surprise and I think I was ready to grab his hand in agreement, but then, quite quickly whilst he continued to explain the job I thought what was I to do about Patrick? I mentioned this to Tony and he generously said "think about the offer and let me know tomorrow".

This was a tough one as I knew that whilst the PPS was the lowest rung on the ministerial ladder it was a great upward leap when you worked alongside a charismatic and active moving young Minister like Tony but then Patrick had confidence in me and I also knew, confidentially, that he was having some medical troubles, which ultimately caused a deterioration in his condition so I said no to Tony and with some sadness. He in turn was fine about it and said "continue to make a success of the Technology Committee".

I had to organise a visit to the Comicom countries – a group of states in Eastern Europe with half a dozen Labour MPs including the likes of Will Owen (later suspected of offloading confidential material) Austin Albu (a former Minister) and Will Howie (a very tough and demanding Scot). It was vastly enlightening to meet and share with the leadership of the five countries on issues of technology with a strong political emphasis. As a group we were welcomed wherever we went. However, security was still an issue, and Will Howie would return to our hotel in Warsaw and pointedly address the massive chandelier "we are back and you can turn your machines on again shitface". The other, Will Owen, a left winger had serious vision problems and I had to walk alongside him on many occasions. However, back in London, the national security officers gave me, as group chairman, a grilling on whether I knew who Will might have met and when, and whether he was absent at night. All very interesting I am sure but I had very little to say except to say that Will was in poor condition and he could hardly see where we were going and when. The grilling concluded but the security were clearly disappointed.

Bulgaria at that time in 1969, presented a sinister appearance. Their government put each member of the group by himself in a long black car with curtains but we had little time to meet fellow parliamentarians or even see the sights.

Romania was rather more normal and I suppose we all felt at ease in Hungary and Poland. I think we did a good job by the time we returned to brief our Ministerial team back in London.

On a totally different parliament trip I made in London with two other new Labour MPs, Alan Le Williams and Stanley Henig to spend an evening at the "glittering" Playboy Club. Obviously not a place we would ever enter on our pay role but we accepted with our ever curious wives (much to the surprise of club organisers!) When we arrived we discovered that the Playboy had lined up female companions with the task of explaining to us why the Club was nothing but a simple (gambling) environment and not in any way breaking the law. It was a rare night off for us and as the wives were given, on entry, a featured place, with some chips and a run of the tables and we MPs were directed to a meeting with the executive to discuss "gambling and the Playboy philosophy!. That lasted an hour and then we were introduced in a smaller alcove for drinks and food. Stanley and Alan were in their cubicles and I sat surrounded by food and actress Sharon Tate. She, a world traveller and film star, talked easily about her films, Valley of the Dolls (1967) which I had to confess, even a keen cinema goer, I had not seen but I knew she was married to Roman Polanski a remarkable if controversial film director. She said "my life is a tangled mess" as I was not sure I had heard her correctly she repeated it. But it still did not make much sense as she was quite beautiful to look at (as I told my wife and anyone else who was desperate to know and there were many). But the glamour of Tate, I felt, did not disguise her vulnerability. I learned later, in fact, that she had fallen in love with film start Christopher Jones and that she was to divorce Polanski so she could be with Jones after filming "Ryan's Daughter" (which I regarded as a fine film). Her new partner apparently also had a tangled life. Apart from Sharon he had just finished dating another actress and was under much pressure from his ex-wife Susan Strasberg. I have always been a fair listener for a good story and Sharon just piled on all the most extraordinary trials of her life "what should I do" she asked me. At this point I was beginning to lose the plot but I managed to eat, drink and say "please go on!" It was a wonderful evening not quite what the Playboy Club expected, not what my wife had expected, but it was massively different from my constituent's complaints. A truly terrible footnote to my story must be that shortly after our meeting Sharon Tate was murdered in a bizarre setting at Charles Manson's California home. This, I found quite unnerving.

Constituency work provided me with real insights into the problems and issues of families and of the economic difficulties they faced. There were, however, a few surprises. I operated an advice centre (now quite standard but in 1966-67 much less so) and I started doing this with a local councillor but it soon became obvious that I was having to deal with a constituent's problems, and the councillor's interference related to his particular problems whilst the constituents would look on rather startled, so I decided to see constituents alone. Perhaps a risk, as I discovered one night in Billericay. The weather was appalling but the few families had been seen by me and I noticed one middle aged lady letting the other families go ahead of her until she was my last case. After the usual greetings and I asked what I could do for her she started in on an extraordinary tale beginning with "I owe my electricity bill". Well that was in no way unusual but then the shock came a moment later when I asked her how much and she replied £12,000. She did not appear to be moved by telling me this and despite my concern I found her behaviour most troubling. Her story was brief "there was a misunderstanding, no bills had been received, we live in that part of the New Town at the very edge and even the mail does not turn up". After a series of questions all of which hardly surprised her, I said I would, of course, get in touch with the electricity executive of the authority as it was such a very large amount. She insisted that she did not want me to use her name! I pointed out that I would try and protect her position but it might be difficult. After long discussions with the electricity authority it appeared that it was not as entirely straightforward as first explained. They had not billed her because she was not on their list. In short, someone had connected her supply to a nearby installation or factory. It sounded absolutely bizarre but the authorities were less shocked than I was. I then spent a further two meetings warning the constituent of the consequences if this connection had been made and I had to ask her whether anyone in her family had tampered with the connection which she denied. A sum was agreed to be paid and the amount was reduced as the result of my pleas to the Authority Chairman. I did offer a warning yet again to her. She expressed ignorance and complete denial of any wrongdoing. She showed little appreciation of my efforts, asking me "why didn't the authority drop all charges so we could start afresh?"

“Receiving the OBE from Her Majesty The Queen, 1994.

“Concluding late night meeting with Palestinian Leader Yasser Arafat, London 1997.”

Namibia. Staff and volunteers following the last session of state wide economic planning. 1994-96.

With Israeli Likud Party Leader (now Prime Minister) Benjamin Natanyahu, Jerusalem 1992.

"International Assistance Leadership Programme. India, 1980."

"A lighter moment with Israel's Foreign Minister
Tzipi Livni, Israel circa 2006. "

"Awaiting boat to return to Cephalonia following earthquake, 1953."

"A most happy day! Everton FC win the FA Cup with Centre-Forward Duncan Ferguson, 1995."

BASILDON AND BILLERICAY

Being a marginal seat – a majority of just over one thousand with the largest electorate in Britain (110,000) I was, I suppose a soft option for the various campaigns to confront an MP yet I coped. One campaign caused me some concern and amusement. It came about as a result of a bill presented by Leo Abse concerning parental rights in cases of abortion. I was sympathetic to the aims of what Leo, a great social campaigner, was trying to achieve but I had not come to any conclusion. A week before the bill was to be voted on I received a delegation from a group of Catholic churches at my advice centre. We had a sober, serious discussion which surprised me as I knew emotions could be easily enflamed in that area of religion and politics. I promised to look into some of the difficulties they posed and they left. Hardly five minutes had gone by and there was a tap at the office door. A head came round the door. It was the priest in the group "sorry to trouble you but silly me, we forgot to leave this petition with you" as he handed it over to me he smiled "you don't need to count the names, there are 1,050". He knew my majority was 1,049.

I had to admire the style and chutzpah of the delegation!

At any rate, other circumstances intervened during the days prior to the vote and I supported Leo Abse. A cynical colleague said to me later "and that is why you will lose your seat in 1970!"

Many constituents began to appreciate my efforts in pursuing their claims or problems but you still had to come up with a smile at receiving this.

Dear Mr Moonman

The speech you made on industrial policy last week was interesting and a load of tripe and onions. I hope that at the next election the people will not hesitate to throw you out good and proper. You and your party will be no loss.

Thank you kindly for reading this.

Yours sincerely

Polite and straight to the point!

A different campaign was the negative, almost anti-Semitic issue that occurred in 1968 to try to restrict the Jewish form of animal slaughter known as "shechita". I approached Peter Archer a non-Jew (a later Solicitor General) to speak, as it was a 10 minute rule bill with only one speaker to oppose. It had little chance of succeeding but there was quite a campaign from a variety of MPs, some concerned, but very hassled by a few anti-Semitic MPs and a big campaign outside the House. It brought me into contact with all manner of pressures. The bill was defeated that day to a fine presentation by Peter Archer a devout Christian.

Often Parliament is seen by outsiders as a place where all ideas flourish, often described as the 'Ideas Factory' but in reality fresh imaginative ideas are more likely to start elsewhere, maybe in think tanks, specialist committees, etc. In fact, much that happens in Parliament is likely to be predictable as are the debates and the speeches by government and opposition. It behoves an MP who is interested at all in fresh inspirational ideas to have a clear idea as to where and how he uses his outside experience or where he obtains his information. I was lucky to have many talks at meetings with Alvin Toffler at an early stage in his writings. Alvin was already a distinguished author and leader of the movement around Future Shock. I had talked with him about the British Institute of Management and management in Britain and he invited me to read a draft of his book. It was a fascinating treatise, he called it a study of "man's bewilderment in the face of accelerating change". Alvin had been an editor of Fortune and a Washington correspondent.

Alvin showed that such is the nature in the speed of social change that it is essential it is properly coordinated and managed otherwise whether in central government planning or local planning we are likely to be the loser. He and I had spoken that change not properly introduced would make many people feel disorientated. The symptoms were already apparent with increasing apathy, depression producing erratic swings in personality and society. Sometimes we met at his home in Mayfair, close to the US Embassy and often in the House of Commons.

It gave me a focus when dealing with Parliament and its sub-culture. I could use some of Alvin's ideas in our debates. I also felt delighted when he asked for my advice before Future Shock was published, signing my copy "to Eric whose concern for tomorrow is evident!" That certainly gave me impetus and a challenge!

At this time and later, my reading and enthusiasm was not only centred on politics and government. When I look at my book shelves the most consistent writers are: Philip Roth, (the Counterlife, Portnoy's Complaint and Goodbye Columbus); Bernard Malamud (The Assistant, The Fixer, The Tenant); Mordecai Richler and Patrick White (Voss and Riders in the Chariot)

It was an exciting period because I often met the authors and their families as I did with Alan Sillitoe (Saturday Night and Sunday Morning and/The Death of William Posters)

I thought it strange when meeting other MPs socially at or in the tea room that their conversation and stance was invariably political but always about plots and plotting. Their cultural life seemed out of reach. The fact that often art and culture were intertwined was hardly mentioned. Anyone reading Patrick White could hardly ignore the remarkable images he created in words and the paintings of Sidney Nolan's beautiful, meaningful illustrations.

There was an exception to the conversation plots in the tea room which was to talk about the sporting success or otherwise of the local football team.

Funnily enough, my own commitment to sport and Everton FC I kept to myself –it was just too personal to have a debate on the Saturday before a game.

My interest in the Beatles was the same, although I did persuade Bessie Braddock to get me into the Christmas Liverpool Empire concert before they became super stars. I learned quickly that it was impossible to tell how good the four were as from the moment the concert began to the close, the passion and volume of the fans' screaming was intense, emotional and total!

Brian Epstein was the gifted businessman who played a large part in the Beatles' success and I knew him as the friendly unassuming proprietor of a well-supported record and music shop in the centre of the city.

As the 1966-70 parliament came to a close, I had to learn the first harsh lesson of politics – as others had done: to win is fantastic but if the public turned their thumbs down on your efforts then it is tough and you go. The departure "arrangements" from the Commons were swift and surgical. The sergeant at arms gave you a friendly note but the details were clear as you had no more than two days to pack up and be off the site so in a frantic few hours we crammed all packages, files, clothes into a hired van and we were gone.

The media hardly seemed to mind that I was the loser as they besieged me and others for comments on: "how badly we felt"; "did it hurt?", "how did your family take it?" At least a reporter who I knew quite well did take the trouble to shake my hand saying, "I'll see you again!" Another less charitable reporter provoked me to say "get stuffed"!

So again I was in the business of chasing a job. I tried to fantasise about going into football or work in the arts, but politics was deep in me, yet I would need to find short term employment fairly quickly until a future election. I soon found that the short-term job for an exMP did not come easily. After all, an employer was unlikely to recruit someone who could hardly provide stability to a firm as he might chase every by-election. I was not inclined to pursue another seat but I could understand an employer's doubts. I had built up friends and many relationships with the Essex constituency and there was lots of pressure for me to stay around and fight in the future and this left me with a good feeling despite my despair at being out of the Commons.

At this time I was irritated by little things on the train to London for instance. Travelling from first (an MPs perk) to standard was a tough one in journeying from Essex to London. I sat alongside many who wanted me out. In fact I would use the car, or even on the occasional trips pay the extra fare, knowing that this depression would not last for very long.

Fortunately and out of the blue, Bill Rodgers a former Minister called me to say that he was working for a group of head hunters and they might be interested to see me. I was delighted and surprised to get the nod from Bill as whilst we had not been buddies we did share some common interests. The job was with an American educational company, Scholastic International to establish a European HQ in London and to set up a facility, fairly immediately to co-ordinate and help with the planning of courses for American graduate students going on to study courses throughout Europe.

With my continued interest in all things American I was keen to follow up the lead. I met the Scholastic president and he seemed enthusiastic to employ me. He was aware that as an active politician I would want to fight the next election but I assured him that if successful I would give it everything I had and would establish the structures they required. I would establish an office from scratch with suitable staff, a local education officer as well as a couple of people to handle the operational side. The summer programme would extend to many parts of Europe and Africa. I was made aware that, on occasion I would need to journey with little notice as happened when a plane load of American high school students arrived in Athens with "problems". This occurred when on one of the programmes, the US plane flew to Athens and I was alerted late on a Saturday night that a young female student was in a very nervous state of agitation and unfortunately the authorities had her admitted to a local psychiatric hospital. I took the early morning flight to Greece and negotiated with the officials that as I was the Director she should be released and booked her into a hotel whilst her father flew in. The hospital was in a dreadful condition and it was essential I acted with speed as she was related to an American congressman and his office was already on the telephone non-stop for me to act; it did not end there as the congressman alerted the US Ambassador in Greece and at the time, it seemed he would not relent, even calling an official at the White House. The job in the main was much less hectic and the opportunity to build up programmes in Russia, Africa and Europe was a welcome diversion from my loss in Parliament.

On my long journeys I made for the company I was able to reflect on what I might do in the future; in other words my long term objective in parliament figured very strongly but I also recognised that parliamentary life was precarious and even if I was able to return at a future election I could still be on the outside at a later age. So I thought it was necessary to keep up with previous interests and skills. So much was happening in management theory and practice I had to keep abreast of change but also my first experience of being an MP made me aware of the strengths and the limits of government policy in relation to industry.

Two books that I wrote subsequently summed up my ideas and the work I had been involved in. The writing was initially tough but I was soon able to get my ideas on paper. I had been forced to neglect my writing whilst an MP with all the constituency commitments. In 1970, Tavistock published my research into the issues surrounding company growth. This was the research I originated and conducted at the University of Manchester in the form of a case study in action research "Communication in an Expanding Organization" (1970). What provoked much public and political interest was the procedures I laid down as a basis for management to be prepared to take initiatives in improving communication in the work place and the establishment of consultation machinery. Some years later this particular formula of communication was introduced into an American textile group.

The book made only a modest impact in this country but sold incredibly well in Japan and thereby hangs a tale. By an accident at the printers and display team in Japan they ran the cover with "my pic" but with an overprint of a long standing Japanese philosopher. If it was me then I resembled an extra in "The Mikado". Of course, they withdrew the cover but as a result of the earlier edition I acquired lively fan mail whilst others accused me of impersonation.

I was a reluctant author of a second book but I was encouraged to write and publish in the late 70s "The Alternative Government" on the issues of power play outside parliament and the way certain businessmen attempted to re-shape government thinking and policy. But the real scope for the book came in a number of talks I had with the former Prime Minister Harold Wilson. This usually took place in the voting lobbies of the Commons when he was no long sought by MPs. A funny thing you simply could not get near to the PM in office, but once he was no longer the top man you could sit and talk easily and frankly. I was pleased to find out that Harold looked forward to our "snatches" of conversation. Otherwise the former Prime Minister would sit quietly in the lobby area whilst the votes were being counted.

We also talked about Merseyside (his constituency being Huyton) and to my delight he wanted to keep in touch with the current performance of Everton FC. He was a sympathetic supporter. He was most knowledgeable about Israel and the Jewish people and told me of his son who had spent some time in the kibbutz movement there.

Harold also relished the chance to share confidences. He told me of his friendship with the then Israeli Ambassador who would frequently respond to Harold's late evening phone call to come along to No. 10 and share a bottle of a good quality whisky.

The Alternative Government was eventually published in 1984. Harold wrote the introduction and he chaired the launch of the book in the Royal Society of Arts. In his introduction he said something which few parties in opposition would hardly recognise or accept:

"Unlike the governing parties of countries, right or left, with authoritarian and usually monopolistic governments and parliament, a British Government, Labour or Conservative, has not merely to win elections so that it can remain seated on the Treasury Benches or Mr Speaker's right hand: it has to move with the times – going beyond and sometimes repudiating some of the policies on which it had won the previous elections".

The former Prime Minister warmly supported my conclusions when I stressed that the alternative government is a continuous process. For a confident, ambitious, political party the time spent in Opposition should be considered precious. It should be a time for examining and assessing procedures and for suggesting improvements as well as for forward planning of policy. It is also an opportunity for building up communications systems with the electorate. It is a time that must not be wasted.

The 1974 election came soon enough and I was back at Westminster. I had the mistaken view that this was likely to be a permanent move. My majority had increased to over 10,000 and there was a new found confidence in the party. As a former MP I was soon active in following up my earlier interests. I had led many campaigns against Scottish devolution (first time round), and in relation to government involvement in collective bargaining, and for greater facilities for the mentally ill and disabled (first Parliamentary chair), schechita, and human rights. Eventually the campaigns caused the Chief Whip to say, "I don't know whose side you're on. But we can't be too careful - you're promoted." But it did not take long for the public to be uncertain indeed suspicious of Labour and its promises. Harold Wilson sadly was unable to carry on due to ill health although he tried desperately to perform his duties.

The new incumbent, lacking Harold's brain power and his feel for everyday situations, was something short of a disaster, as was evident when he failed to call a General Election in September 1978 against the advice and reasoning of a large majority of the Parliamentary Labour Party. His failure to do so meant that Labour was clobbered with all the issues of the 1978-79 Winter of Discontent. Callaghan clung to power and was responsible for the many subsequent years of Labour opposition. This is summed up in his much quoted comment (which of course he later denied) as he stepped off a holiday plane answering reporters on the economic downturn, "Crisis – what crisis?" Many of the young MPs paid the price for his ego. "Smiling

Jim" was more disliked even despised by all those who lost their seats, myself included, because he clung to office in that Autumn when Labour's election machinery was primed and ready to go, which was deactivated with the bashing in those winter months. I wrote to the Prime Minister in the September to urge action and avoid the industrial strife as did many young MPs whose understanding and street feel was considerably greater than the Prime Minister's and that of his advisors. However, I have since learned that he made the decision to stay until the following year without reference to anyone. Rather typical because it meant that a generation and more of Labour politicians were isolated and as we know, the party did not recover for ever so much longer.

So I lost my seat. Many of my colleagues were inclined to say "that's it" let's go back to what we were doing, whether in teaching, business or simply leave the country. I certainly did not fancy the latter option but I wanted some freedom to act whilst some political opportunity could come again. Only later did I realise that the odds of this happening in the short term were remote.

CLOCKING ON IN THE HEALTH SERVICE

I was working on a temporary basis as a researcher in a small establishment and my boss the Director was far from being a happy bunny. Yet the 70 year old guy was adored by his two senior secretaries – and so on his birthday they assembled all the senior staff in a room with a large birthday cake in the middle on the table whilst we awaited to sing his greetings. We were asked to sit and wait and as a half hour went by the outer door to the room revealed he had arrived. The two ladies went to him and then there was initially muffled voices increasingly agitated ("I am not going in there") but then louder voices by all three. More waiting time whilst we looked on at the cake and then the door opened: the Director put his head round the door and said "hello" with little cheer and was not seen again that night. Never give a long-standing employee a surprise party.

After a few months one or two areas of work came up which seemed to provide an opportunity. One was to take on the chairmanship of a health authority in my own borough of Islington and which included the Whittington Hospital (well used by my three children) and I suppose this invitation reflected what I had accomplished as chair of the Mental Health Parliamentary Committee and on health issues generally, and so I was quick to accept.

Like other jobs I have done in my life I put a lot of energy into the work as well as some political acumen. I was well supported with a splendid former headmaster, Ron Lendon and a solicitor Ivor Walker a former Camden councillor as Board members. All three of us were of the Left but it was not an issue in public service – in a hospital at that – to run a successful hospital. We ran a tight ship, kept to budget even if the public meetings were often a political joust stimulated by the various public and union representatives. Because the public meetings at the neighbouring health authority in Hackney collapsed in disorder as the chair ordered the union representation out (there was a near riot with chairs flung about and fists flying at all the members). The Regional health chair insisted a drastic tightening up of security in "these difficult times". In Islington I had managed to get through the monthly public meetings pretty well but the Region insisted otherwise so that we had two Alsatian dogs to help me! The 80 or so people who attended were none too pleased but fortunately the handlers prevented the dogs growling, otherwise I might have been the first victim as the animals looked suspiciously at me throughout the meeting and I did not fancy my chances!

One issue did make the headlines and arose when Labour's shadow Health minister Michael Meacher foolishly circulated a questionnaire to all Labour chairmen of Health Authorities demanding to know the political affiliations of members. I complained privately to the party leader, Neil Kinnock who did not disagree that the request was an error so promised to deal with the issue. As time went by with little action, the Guardian ran a story from a number of chairmen pointing out Michael Meacher's error of judgement. Ultimately and with no further action from Kinnock or his deputy, despite further representations by me, I resigned from the party (to rejoin several months later) as the Times stated:

"Had I followed the advice of colleagues and thrown Mr Meacher's demand in the bin I would have been indirectly endorsing the latest efforts by Labour's left wing". On this occasion, (the shadow health spokesman) attempted to mandate Labour members of statutory bodies to vote "in accordance with party dictates"; it was an error of judgement. My objection was clear. This was a threat to an individual's rights but also an unfortunate way for Labour to deal with the consequent damage in the public eye. Mr Meacher was a fool. Members of local health authorities who were also Labour party members were asked on House of Commons paper, to record, for the benefit of Mr Meacher, details of the sex, age, political affiliation and voting habits of all members of the authority.

I did not know the politics of, for instance the nursing or GP representatives on the Islington health authority. Nor did I wish to know.

As Mr Meacher went public on television, I also vigorously argued the point with the media asking what will Mr Meacher do with the information. Will Labour members who do not tow the party line be replaced by others more willing to be puppets? And what of those who belong to no party? This was already way over the calamity line.

I was aware that the process had already been applied to Labour members of school governing bodies in at least the Inner London Education area.

With the result of this dispute I received massive support from many in the health service and the Labour Party and petitions were started in supporting me. Many Labour MP's felt that Labour was still obsessed with control and not about forming a caring administration. For the Tories it was a propaganda boost.

Surprise, surprise. Neil Kinnock eventually responded and warned Meacher to back down. Privately Kinnock told me that he felt that Meacher was treating this as a censoring exercise but he should not present it as Labour's.

The issue caused merriment in some quarters. Alan Watkins in the Observer wrote (18 Nov 1984) "Mr Moonman would have protested more effectively if he had advised Mr Meacher to jump off the terrace into the Thames and made this advice known to the press."

An even more extraordinary twist occurred when in commenting on the case in the Observer there were questions about the intentions and motives of Meacher's behaviour and a high Court action followed. Anthony Howard deputy editor of the paper said he felt "total bewilderment" about Meacher's action. The case lasted four days and covered many aspects of Meacher's life and background. A lunch took place with the Observer editor at the Guy Hussar restaurant at Meacher's request but failed to resolve the dispute. I should mention that I was not invited but I was a standby witness and I received a kindly note and a cheque from the Observer!

At any rate, following further talks with Labour colleagues I did return to the party after a few months and the Meacher questionnaire was never implemented.

In the same year on a more creative but totally different issue I wrote a Financial Times article on supporting and resourcing the NHS considerably more than hitherto, "The annual budgets were a political ping pong between the parties".

And I explained: "The debate over the National Health Service is all too often confined to an agonising call for more resources. Yet in spite of the creation of the NHS 40 years ago no rational basis exists to define what the resource requirement should be."

Still relevant today, some years on, "Resources have never been matched to the health needs of the community. What has been lacking is a co-ordinated strategy taking into account variations in regional and district requirement and, where resources are limited, alternative methods of funding". (Financial Times Aug 17, 1985).

Then, as now, there are only a few funding choices. General taxation accounts for 95 per cent of NHS revenue; another way of obtaining national taxes would be to earmark certain sums, such as a proportion of income tax rates or a new tax on the lines of VAT or national Insurance for the NHS.

I followed the articles up with this appeal at an NHS seminar: "Another level of choice is the distribution of finance – between the NHS and the private sector as well as the allocation between regions and between districts. The controversial question of waiting lists could be met head on by helping district health authorities buy services from other districts and sell them on a much wider scale than now."

In my many walks around the Whittington and other hospitals I became aware of a critical gap in perception between the varied levels of staff and how this affected staff-patient communication.

Here my experiences in public service and parliament triggered me to try to get closer to the consumer (the patient). I decided on an advisory centre similar to my MP's surgery in the constituency. Also I should say I felt comfortable in relating to the public in this way. Of course I met with all manner of objections from senior staff and also from several local councillors who asked my chief executive "what is the chairman up to?" No matter, I found support from all parts of the service which was encouraging. I did make it clear that if I was confronted with any form of a medical issue I would immediately be in touch with the responsible head of department or his or her deputy. With that assurance the idea worked well. It was a fortnightly session of one hour but usually it ran on much longer.

After a year I did get a number of previous critics to change their mind about my clinic. In deference to some doctors I did not use the term "surgery".

In the main, the public came with serious or worrying matters and I genuinely believe the format worked well. But not always! Once I received a delegation of orthodox Jewish women from nearby Stamford Hill. They came to the point straight away. They wanted to light their candles in the ward on the Sabbath night and ensure their dietary rules could be protected. I could not agree to the naked flame on the ward but they persisted and eventually they dropped their persuasive English to a dubious Yiddish which I understood (a second language in my boyhood home). But I thought it best to look bemused and whilst their feelings about me, in consequence, were pretty low and insulting, I smiled and ushered them out. Perhaps they found out later I could understand the language equally well. In fact Yiddish is an ideal language if you wanted to swear as Lita Epstein said "if you can't say anything nice, say it in Yiddish".

Another surgery session brought me in touch with a complete odd ball who calmly announced as he sat down that he was dissatisfied with one consultant in particular and (a short delay...) "I want to kill him". I gulped, smiled, but he was having none of it. I tried to talk the man through his evident hostility, even resorting to the suggestion that "it would be unhelpful to do such a terrible thing to the doctor's other patients, particularly as we are so understaffed in the hospital". To be on the safe side with such a very determined patient, I brought into our session our senior security officer who, combined with my efforts we achieved some headway as the man promised not to take any action and left crying. We did, however, keep an eye on him and informed the psychiatric services and of course the consultant concerned!

After several sessions, a number of health professionals and social service providers who were resident in the district also came to see me. I expected to hear about the shortage of resources and their inability to do the job they were trained and paid for. No, many did more than that – they argued that respective governments and the political parties passed the buck from one to the other. They were most troubled. I summed up their concerns as best I could: I agreed often the long range problems were never tackled in the Health Service with the result that resource shortages were passed from one government to the next. At the same time, service demands were increasing dramatically as we live longer with evidence of newer diseases, such as AIDS and other costly treatments. It was not merely increasing resources but also the need for a critical well devised strategy. All their points were legitimate areas of argument between the political parties. Yet they did not start with a common set of statistics and I had to admit that their political prejudice took over. The answer lay in an independent body respected by all sides which would attempt an accurate assessment of resources. It was a fantastic discussion and we agreed to meet regularly, which we did.

Chairing the health services had been a demanding public assignment but I could still say after 13 years a most rewarding one. How to lighten your load? I never gave much thought to this as I went around the wards or the A and E. But prior to one annual staff party the organiser said to me, "could you make your presentation funny and light?" So I started to reflect on the odd ball things that can go wrong in the daily life of a hospital and taking the mickey out of the high powered status consultants and my own limitations. It went very well indeed!

INTERNATIONAL RED CROSS NAMIBIA

Almost immediately following the end of my term of office at the Whittington I received an invitation from the International Red Cross to visit Namibia to help to prepare a social/economic plan that was becoming increasingly necessary in Africa.

Africa was a rewarding experience despite the pressures from the sponsors, the International Red Cross, to complete an expanding project to the original brief. The staff and the Africans we helped were wonderfully friendly and grateful for the advice and support we provided.

The project had a several years span. There was a queue of people often waiting in the Windhoek office in the early morning. It may not have been part of the original brief but we never ignored the requests to help, to talk, to explain. It was clear that change was happening in this culture but many were not prepared for it.

Many of the population were not adequately informed or trained for the opportunities which could emerge. A large scale educational and skills programme was essential and I planned for its introduction.

After a while the Red Cross also asked me to visit the office in Harare. Remarkably there was a small Jewish community and they discovered that I was in the country and that I was a former British MP and a Jew. I was asked to speak to the community one night in the synagogue. Prior to the meeting I was invited to the chairman's home for dinner. I arrived in a taxi only to find a gated entrance and despite all our efforts to open the substantial open the substantial gates, they could not, due to the regular power cuts. The family emerged from the house to explain that this was the result of the sudden but inevitable and increasing power cuts in Zimbabwe, as the economy was woeful and many services were down, so we waited on either side of the gates. Nothing happened and as the lecture time approached, I was grateful when the young teenage son slipped a chocolate bar through the slats to me. Eventually with little time to go, the father managed to work his way through a rear door and we got to the synagogue with a large audience but no power and no lights. Improvisation and the chocolate bar was the order of the day, as I had a choice to cancel or talk in the dark! I chose the latter as I was due to leave Zimbabwe the next day. But there was a further improvisation as torches were provided for those sitting in the front two rows who flashed their lights on my face! It was the most extraordinary experience in all my years of speaking – and, I continued to be concerned if the torch batteries would run out! Some did but it did not matter as it was the most enthusiastic audience I have ever had.

Like many countries in Africa, Namibia had neglected planning its management and operation infrastructures. This had produced a certain reluctance for outside companies to invest and divert operations within the country. However, several senior government officials recognised this failure and decided to engage in a long range project to improve training and social services.

I spent three months in each of three years in the country and remained in contact during the rest of the time.

By returning each year it was possible to discern the extent of progress of the plan and the operations. It was important to gain local confidence and I believe I succeeded by the responses and commitment made to me at the highest level by the President's office. It was ultimately deemed a success with the President attending the final session.

Returning to the UK, and outside health issues, I spent my time helping in the creation of a group to monitor and publicise the extent of growing racism, with particular emphasis on sport. This was established as the Centre for Contemporary Studies. Having been a football fan all my life, it troubled me when increasingly at that time in the 80s some fans abused minority groups at the game. There were many incidents, a word shouted out at a player – or more menacingly fighting against other supporters if they saw black people in the crowd.

FIGHTING RACISM

Some friends and I decided to raise funds to put together a research group to highlight the dangers and awaken public concern. Up to that time there was scant recognition of the way racism had entered the football game.

In the early research we soon realised that it was going to be difficult to isolate sport from society as a whole so any enquiries had to be broadly based. The centre operated modestly in a small room with some chairs and a desk but we were helped enormously when industrialist Gerald Ronson offered us a larger space and telephone facilities in one of his buildings. He himself had an impressive track record opposing anti-Semitic groups as a young man in East London

I gave the centre a fair amount of my free time. We had put together a good supportive advisory group including Professor Hilde Himmelweit, Sir David Price, Nancy Seear and Peter Shore MP.

Our first report received an encouraging press which brought in a number of supporters. After describing the sports scene in one report we then tackled the political pressures in universities (May 1983). The paper examined some of the consequences of universities' increasing dependence on "private" funds. Inevitably in some cases, he who pays the piper will want to call the tune: the relationship between the universities and the sources of finance whose funds they solicit is one of crucial importance to those who care for the future of the British university and its standards of independence. That relationship may not yet give sufficient cause for alarm but we provided some crucial evidence to make these issues known.

Another paper covered by an American colleague, Professor Yonah Alexander (June 1986) dealt with violence and terrorism. He described low intensity warfare and his conclusion attracted much attention:

"The failure of the international community to fully recognise terrorism as criminal behaviour and as low intensity warfare has encouraged the growth of terrorist activity in the last two decades. The statistics of terrorist violence are, indeed staggering. From 1970 to 1985, 25,381 domestic and international terrorist incidents occurred. A total of 47,560 individuals have been killed and another 29,769 wounded with property damage estimated at several billions of dollars".

So what began as a commentary on racism, moved into general violence and even international terrorism. Perhaps this was inevitable but I kept a close watch that we did not lose our bearings and the point of our initial setting up. In addition to the reports we published, the Centre received dozens of enquiries each month on racism in our society and sport in particular.

Thus far, it would seem I have only been concerned with working and exploring opportunities in large operations and services in confronting problems. Not so; it has been an essential part of my work that I am able to work alongside people in need and on a personal level. Perhaps this reflects my Jewish upbringing and roots whereby we aim to a standard of performing a mitzvah (services) to help and aid those in need. In recent years, this commitment has been extended into a national mitzvah day yet it is deeply rooted in our theology and as a daily guide to perform.

THE LOVE OF MITZVAH

I undertook a particular interest and concern in supporting families who had suffered bereavement.

I am reminded of the importance of mitzvah – to help each other at all times – and its importance for being a Jew. I have been fortunate to learn from many Rabbis whilst attending Shabbat services in the small Southport community with my wife, Gillian and also in the large congregation in Belsize Square, London.

The Jewish religion takes the death of family and friends most seriously and I have always taken my family responsibilities with care. I am often asked why this care of the deceased? Probably a three generation matter. My late father Borach would often be called in, following his retirement, to help to wash the deceased and commit prayers for them. It is a single honour within the religion to do this. It requires great diligence and care and here he was a most thoughtful choice to undertake the honour.

Whilst I have not been personally called to perform in this mitzvah (honour), I have never ignored the responsibilities in the care of cemeteries and I make many visits throughout the months to ensure that the family masonry is in good working order. Indeed I had an arrangement with the local stonemason to follow up other graves in need of some repair and then I would follow up to inform the next-of-kin.

My son Josh seems to have taken on concerns and mitzvah even further. Josh has served in many parts of the world with Kenyon, a company dealing with aid and support following natural disasters. He also served in Ground Zero in New York.

I also found much satisfaction in working on a one to one relationship in mentoring. One concerned an upstanding woman in Islington who had been forced out of a job yet her admirers were enormous in number.

Anna Scher created a terrific dance academy, a "fame school" in Islington. Many children would rush from day school to find their way to the building off the Caledonian Road. They learned acting skills and the power of the voice, techniques that build confidence. Anna's enthusiasm and skills launched the careers of many TV and film stars. Clearly she was a personality in her own right but she took ill and visiting her I discovered that a couple of her board trustees were going to make changes to the academy without her approval including her removal so she hit the buffers with the bureaucrats and was utterly distressed. Unfortunately her likely supporters shocked by those events had resigned which left Anna isolated so I began a campaign in support of her. In a very short time we had hundreds of friends and pupils signed up to get her reinstated supported by the likes of Hollywood star Michael Caine and Martin Luther King's family.

Despite public meetings and a great wealth of local Islington support (and well beyond) the bureaucrats would not give way, offering Anna only limited teaching time. A further indignity came when they dropped Anna's name from the building. We could not win her return but with such outside support and with Anna's determination and her many theatre friends we helped to set up "Anna in Exile" classes at a local church in Copenhagen Street, Islington. She had found her students, her confidence and again is the star of Islington.

Interestingly the "Fame School" in the United States sent their good wishes. The Islington Council, ignoring those who forced her out, honoured her with the Freedom of the Borough and later she received a further honour: this outstanding spirited teacher received the MBE. Her school continues and thrives!

Politics apart, and my involvement as a "macher" (a person who takes initiatives) I wanted to share my experience and personal development with and personal development with young people who had perhaps started uncertainly in life, like myself, people who were now working to enhance their skills and ambitions.

Even at Toynbee Hall University Settlement, where I lived in the fifties and sixties, I recognised how deeply some boys in their late teens suffered anguish because of their poor domestic circumstances Often in a one-parent family, that parent could work away for weeks at a time and this resulted in the youth not having the confidence to try to push on in their life. When I met with one young man who I helped to guide over a period of three years he told me something I shall never forget. "I have been short-changed in my life".... We would sit together and I gave him simple exercises in English and public affairs but more important counselling him and monitoring his progress and failures. I admired his increasing confidence when he said "you show pleasure when I get things or issues right and I respect you when you admit to getting matters wrong". We kept in touch long after I left Toynbee and he advanced in so many ways – his jobs, his friendships and ultimately he began his own wife and family.

At university I initially lectured for a time in the areas of management and individual development. I enjoyed the tutorials with the young men and women that came to learn. Such a student was Deepak, initially hesitant in group discussions, he showed a growing interest in issues like "self-discipline" and how to use subject knowledge and succeed personally not just an understanding of issues of self-management and organizational development.

With all mentoring I believe there are some moments when not only does the young person or student have to see an "amber light" to begin a process of awareness or enlightenment but those doing the monitoring need a similar moment, of recognised understanding, when a connection with the student has been made.

This young Sikh rapidly developed in his studies and with awareness of his strengths he is now a Director of a growing business. We do not meet too often now but 20 years on we keep in touch by phone and whenever he feels the need to share experiences.

Then there was a young Nigerian woman who had struggled at school and had difficulty obtaining any form of job to keep her interested. I met her whilst using an internet café and she seemed cheerful and interested whilst typing. I discovered she ran the shop for a guy who had disappeared leaving her with the responsibility – and debts. Daily she was being bombarded with emails and visits from heavies seeking payment and details of the original owner's whereabouts. She had to quit she told me, "but how?". I looked through the papers she may have signed to the owner although it was a mass of contradictions as to who was responsible. We talked around the issues and the alternatives available to her, "you cannot be held responsible and as you are subjected to such pressure and with your management talent (which had over a period impressed me) you should just walk out. She brightened up considerably. She walked to the door of the shop "go on" I said, "don't look back". And that was precisely what she did.

After a month or so I met up with her and suggested some secretarial openings. She was keen on a full time job. She sailed though one interview in a public body. Now years later she has worked up the hierarchy in the company and is a high ranking officer. Her family life has benefitted. We keep in touch when she feels a new management situation is likely to confront her.

There was another young person referred to me by a friend, who believed she had great potential as a sculptress. She had left school at 16 but she lacked the confidence to press her claims and move on to another level in her work.

When I first saw her exhibits I realised it was staggering. Modestly she could not understand my excitement and enthusiasm. She lived simply in a flat in North London. Frances started painting at 8 years of age producing her first one off statues of her father. Not a specialist in sculpture myself yet I could see the undaunted quality and I supported her in not wanting to join the artistic trend towards shocking as exemplified by the likes of Damien Hirst.

She had married and she was ready to concentrate on her two children. Rather than operate widely in the arts field, I decided to help her concentrate where she could make the greatest impact, namely to work in bronze likeness. Utilising some of my contacts she began a series of head busts, many of politicians (the late Sir Bernard Braine) and showbiz personalities such as Harvey Goldsmith.

I also encouraged Frances to perform her work in a public setting to capture the environment and the mood of the locality.

In recent years her work and style have been very much widely accepted and her sittings have included HM the Queen, The Duke of Edinburgh and Prince Charles as well as many who lead in the arts and social fields.

As my hospital and health job came to an end I was able to devote rather more time to a radio station board on which I served as a member. The station, Essex Radio was to broadcast to my old constituency areas of Basildon, Billericay and beyond. The station covered an ideal area for me as I knew it well and I was invited to head up a team of local enthusiasts to help to put in a bid as there could be much competition for the station. We did get the license and I became Chair – it was a news and music station and it was what was called at the time "a legal station" in contrast to Radio Caroline which transmitted off the Essex coast. I made many good friends and there was always a terrific atmosphere amongst the staff, volunteers and friends. We ran for several years with considerable success until a large commercial station started to take over those smaller, and more local stations, and the original team and enthusiasm was gradually eroded.

Still on entertainment which I love - radio and film were fascinating outlets to me and around this time I was invited to represent a more general view of arts at the British Film Institute. The BFI through its cinema the National Film Theatre in Waterloo had been a happy and restful environment for me as Governor. I eventually served two terms with a farewell gift of a generous life long season pass – just about the only presentation I have ever had for public service. There were many experts and cinema "insiders" on the Board of the BFI and it was fascinating to hear their comments and their line of thinking and commitment at meetings. Only two of us came from a different perspective to the professionals we were with and, like my experience in Essex Radio, proved to be invaluable for the projects we now worked on.

Looking back at the eight years I spent at the BFI I realised that, once again I was fortunate to be in a semi-public organisation going through a period of some considerable change. The director was responsible to the Minister of Culture but much of the planning and preparation of schedules was prompted at Board level. One aspect of its work did make the headlines rather more obviously, namely what became the Annual Film Festival and although shown in London the concept was extended to centres in cities and towns throughout the country.

Another chance to work in the arts field occurred later when Gerald Ronson was invited to chair the Natural History Museum's Development operation, at a key time in the general direction and finance of the Museum. He asked me to support the staff and help to create and enhance the Museum's profile and finance.

Her Royal Highness Princess Diana had agreed to become Patron. I worked with her in development policy and PR and without a doubt all things expressed about her are absolutely correct. She was charming, thoughtful and very funny about the Museum's bureaucracy. She saw quickly that "we two are the outsiders" but the development plan worked and she brought in many donors to fund all manner of projects. The chair of the foundation was Gerald Ronson and he wisely invited her for the very special functions. Thus the fundraising campaign was very successful.

Princess Diana was all you could wish for as a "boss". One night I received a phone call at my home from the Director of the Museum confirming that our Patron would be making a totally surprise early morning visit to the museum with her children and also to buy gifts. No press" –the conversation ended. I am sure I fell asleep mouthing "No press".

In the morning at 7.30 am I thought I would ensure that there was no hitch in the arrangements as she was expected at 8.30, but as soon as I left South Kensington tube station I could not help but notice the enormous presence of the press. There they were: All vans, cameras, right up Cromwell Road. The press were on to it!

The visit was a success and there were many images of the Royal party taken at the event. When it was all over I spoke to one of the reporters I knew and said "how in hell's name did you know about the visit, you know it was "hush, hush". He looked at me as if I had lost my marbles. "Diana rang us of course!".

My interest in the Natural History Museum did not end there as I assisted Henry Barlow, a great supporter of the Museum in setting up the Friends of the Museum. It was essential that in addition to the considerable organizational structure and its power base, that there should be an informal approach to the various exhibitions and a welcoming door to the general public. The result was the creation of the Friends – aimed at families, teachers and students.

We wanted to develop a large long term body of loyal members who were keen to support the Natural History Museum through their membership, participation in Museum activities and through helping to raise awareness of its work amongst a wider public both in the UK and abroad.

It was a success and much appreciated by staff over the years. I still get a thrill walking down the main staircase in the early winter evenings.

Gerald Ronson, businessman and philanthropist, was the most remarkable and successful fund-raiser one could imagine. One incident says it all. The museum was rightly concerned that although its development and funding committee was powerful with the most distinguished ladies and gentlemen, many from Kensington, they did not contribute cash themselves. So Gerald Ronson was installed as chairman of this committee. At its first meeting,

Gerald informed them how serious the issue was, and after an inspiring but blunt speech he said "Let's go round the table for your funds – crucially I'll give two and a half grand." The response was less overwhelming than he expected. I was at his side, as he announced, "Eric just record the second round as I'll double mine to five grand. Let's double and treble to save the museum". He looked sober. He continued to achieve the amount he anticipated although I did think one of the contributors clearly was about to have a heart attack. Nevertheless, Gerald beamed. "That is so much better", he said. Gerald then closed the meeting. His subsequent tenure was equally lively and personal.

However, our appointment came to an end. There was a tragic end for the Princess in Paris. and Gerald had his personal problems, making public life difficult.

During a lull in the NHM development programme I was asked whether I would care to assist in sharpening up some of the images of the exhibitions, in particular the dinosaur. The staff were tremendous to work with and I agreed, although it would mean visiting the States and Canada to observe the relevant museum PR programmes. I learned little in Chicago and other museums and I was encouraged to turn to Canada by my NHM brief.

At the border I encountered a problem with a lethargic security officer who asked my business. I explained it was a short visit in connection with dinosaurs. "Are you looking for them?" he said and I replied, "sort of".

At this he awoke from his partial slumber and quickly called for three more officers to look me over "could you say that again, your name is Moonman? You are looking for what?" More officers arrived and there was a mighty queue of visitors who moaned, where I could go or "what is this country coming to letting these cranks in Canada roam around!" Eventually I got through and on my departure back to England I was determined to leave the dinosaurs alone.

The name, Moonman, certainly added to the complications in establishing any credibility in my search for dinosaur remains.

I suppose you can hardly expect an official to understand let alone cope with the guy opposite from Berdichev called Moonman who was originally Munman from a family bakery. (caraway seeds et al.)

I have had a number of surprising moments with the name, sometimes unwelcome, as in my army training with the excessively enthusiastic sergeant major who could concentrate on me his anger rather than on the likes of Smith and Jones.

During my time as an officer at the Board of Deputies, I co-led a hush-hush meeting with the then Palestinian leader Yasser Arafat. It would take place in a hotel room in the late evening and whilst no major policy issue was likely to come up, it was hoped to encourage him to think positively about meeting with the Israeli leadership. It was a time when he was playing hard to get and I was duly warned.

The meeting was not constructive. However, after discovering my name was Moonman, he become light hearted. Whether this had some bearing on his later thinking, I know not. We did, however, make some progress re a meeting with the Israelis. I left, and he linked my arm and murmured "Moonman, Moonman, yes, yes". Nevertheless what was planned to be a brief late night meeting ran into close on one hour and a half.

Another occasion, rather more public, arose when Neil Armstrong the first US astronaut made his initial visit to London. The government laid on a grand Guildhall dinner.

All came to praise the American initiative. The US Ambassador, however, did rather overstate the power of US resources and initiatives. The host, Prime Minister Harold Wilson, a little peeved wound up the drawn-out proceedings and explained in his brief Yorkshire, why we may have a way to go before we in Britain can make a similar project, but in the meantime, we have our own, Moonman in the House of Commons – please stand up Eric!'

It was a crazy moment and many were convinced, that Harold and I had arranged the 'Moonman Finale!' Not so.

Harold's ability to seize the humour from a political 'moment' was well expressed by an incident in 1974 and recalled by Robert Orchard in the Times diary, 'Harold was egged during His 1974 election, the second election that year, at a town hall meeting. With albumen sliding down his suit, the PM said: "During the 1970 election, after six years of a Labour government, someone threw an egg at me. At the election in February, after three years of a Tory government, nobody threw an egg at me. Now, someone has done it again after six months of a Labour government." He paused and added: "It goes to show you can only afford to throw eggs under Labour."

MAKING THE ZIONIST CASE

By 2000 I had been involved with the Zionist movement and Anglo Jewish politics for some years, having served as a senior officer of the Board of Deputies, the communal body of and for Jews in Britain and also as an officer of the Zionist Federation. Now I realised that it was becoming ever more essential to provide guidance for the current and future generations. I was invited to give the Zionist Federation centenary address to a specially convened conference in London. I was delighted to accept and to present my ideas and to offer a likely programme of action.

My colleagues in the Zionist movement and amongst many in the Board of Deputies were anxious to see the role of the various organisations redefined in view of the changes in British society. I took a great deal of trouble with the lecture – not to satisfy every single Jew but to ensure that I produced a coherent and easily identifiable framework which could be related to likely future policies of social change in Britain.

In the light of the years since having held office in the Zionist Federation and as I write now, it seems clear that the issues reviewed all these years ago are still maddeningly relevant.

I employed in my speech the thesis advanced by Walter Laquer a few years back when he argued that "Zionism is a response to anti-Semitism". All national movements have come into existence and developed their specific character in opposition to and usually in the fight against the outside forces". However, in the Jewish religion, Zion as a symbol for the homeland and other mystical factors played a crucial role in the development of Zionism. But political Zionism, as distinct from mystical longings, would have not come into existence but for the precarious situation of central and East European Jewry in the second half of the nineteenth century. It became a psychological necessity for the central European intellectuals, who realized that the emancipation of Jews had triggered off a powerful reaction and who then found the road to full emancipation barred by strong hostile forces. I advanced a brief history on the interaction between Israel and Britain.

In the centenary lecture, I explained that from 1917 to 1948 London was a major centre of the Zionist political struggle led by Dr Chaim Weizmann (President of the Zionist Federation). He became head of the World Zionist Organisation and the first President of Israel (1948-1952). Then there was the leadership of Professor Selig Brodetsky, who was the President of the Board of Deputies (1939-1949). He was also involved with the ZF in the struggle for a Jewish State against powerful anti-Zionist forces within Anglo-Jewry.

For Zionism, in the words of Theodore Herzl at the First Congress at Basle in 1897, was to be a return of the Jews to Judaism even before the return to the Jewish land. The foundation of the English Zionist Federation established at the Basle Congress in August 1897, took place at a time when both externally and internally the Jewish outlook was very sombre. The concluding decade of the nineteenth century appeared as the culmination of the Jewish tragedy that had gathered in force as anti-Semitism in Germany became, in the seventies, a powerfully organised Movement.

In my presentation I stressed that there were three key areas for which I would urge support: first to be actively alert in challenging the growth of anti-Semitism. I did not consider for one moment that this had gone from the minds and attitudes of many people. We must always put this at the forefront of communal decisions and the likely result of controversial policies or incidents in Israel.

Secondly we must never neglect what has been created in Israel. The spirited and cultural centre for Jews has been achieved with love and care. We are its ambassadors.

A third objective for the Zionist Federation is to reach out and involve and welcome non-Jews who were sympathetic to our cause. The spirituality of Judaism and Zionism appeals to many Christians – they can be friends and advocates. We must not ignore their good will and advice.

My lecture was well received and, as a result, the Zionist Federation set up a network and group in every part of Britain. In particular, the third objective to involve many Christian groups was an immediate success with the Christian Friends of Israel.

At another lecture I gave I provoked a different reaction from a member of the audience. This was on February 24th 2000. I was in Southport, in a Jewish centre. After I gave my usual overview of what makes a cohesive community, a young woman then gave me an admirable vote of thanks. She was a former graduate of the very same City University where I continued to have some dealings through the Health Authority and the Department of Health. We chatted and, as they say in the States, I checked her out (as she did me) and we were married a year later. Gosh!

WAYS OF SERVICE

This is not a conclusion. Yet when talking to audiences in recent years I am often asked why I have had so many diverse jobs and "what I will follow it all up with next" or "is there another challenge?" My answer is always yes – but anything rather than suggest retirement. Perhaps it falls naturally to me to continue challenging issues, causes and confronting prejudice because I feel I am still on a learning curve of life but anyone can join in – at whatever age. The voluntary sector is wide open and there are no limits for men and women who want to give something back to society.

One person who understood this learning curve was Sir Sigmund Sternberg, a great philanthropist and communal leader.[1*] He introduced, in co-operation with the Times newspaper, an award for the over 70s. He wanted to encourage people not to await retirement but to develop new areas of service to help the wider community. The Sternberg Life Award has already an impressive list of previous winners:

Dr Colin Murray Parkes, (2011) who has dedicated much of his life to the care of the bereaved; Major John Majendie (2010) a veteran of the Second World War, who organises annual pilgrimages to France for his fellow Normandy veterans; Phoebe Caldwell (2009) for her work in improving the lives of people with severe autism, and the inaugural award in 2008 went to Helen Bamber in recognition of a lifetime dedicated to helping the victims of torture.

[1] * Passed away in October, 2016 since preparing this manuscript

It has been a welcome move by the older generation and the response in general for the award has been most encouraging. I strongly feel that when taking up a new job or experience in later life you should aim somehow to be directly involved in the forming of objectives.

There are two such areas I am committed to that encourage such a learning curve. A few ex MPs like Alan Lee Williams, Joe Ashton and myself attempted to establish some association or meeting-ground having left parliament. We put the proposal to then Speaker, Betty Boothroyd but we were strongly rebuffed. However, at the same time, other former MPs were also pursuing the idea and with the new Speaker Michael Martin, we got the green light to form the Former Member of Parliament Association. We elected a committee and I was responsible for an outreach programme and that offered members the chance to talk to students in the universities and colleges. The Association took off and we soon had signed up 250 members (now 450) including former Prime Ministers and other senior members of the cabinet.

The Association provides a point of entry for past MPs who up to that time (year 2000 +) had no special access to parliament and had to queue with the general public whilst researchers and secretaries with passes sailed through! The Association took up an issue about the level of parliamentary pensions. The Association became similar to sister associations operating over many years in the US Senate and Congress. My brief was a creative one, in as much as I was providing a service to academia by arranging visits to colleges. The aim was not to engage in political knock about but to explain and share questions and answers on current parliament and governance. We have also supported a research project on "Life after Parliament" at Leeds University.

My other practical commitment – as a part of my learning curve – was totally different. I agreed to act as a Trustee of a premier division football club. As a lifelong fan of Everton FC – starting as a wee mite in the boys' pen at Goodison Park, there was no hesitation on my part to join the trustees. The specific concern of the former players' foundation is to assist and welcome players in need once they had completed their time with the club.

Unlike many of today's players earning handsome wages and benefits, the players of the 60s and 70s were left with little to support them in their aging years plus many were prone to damaged limbs through extensive training – and here the association played and still plays a unique role. Everton had set the bar in the care of its former players, yet few clubs have followed the practice. Ex-players also have open access to current fixtures. I have been immensely touched by the appreciation of former players in the help we provide and general care for their health.

I am often asked how does one feel comfortable moving into an organisation's "top table". Surely, they say, if every organisation has its own jargon and specific targets, how does one break rank into the "culture". Of course each organisation will be different, but what I have found is that it is not always about the subject or the technology, but it is about the people. My advice to anyone else in this situation is to brief yourself before attending a first and second meeting. Again, read all you can but supplement that with talking through issues with the senior staff (you will pay them a compliment by calling on them) and at the meeting, take it slowly before you sound off. Do not plunge into the swimming pool if you can hardly swim.

Have my ideas changed on personal development whilst over the years serving on so many diverse bodies? The simple answer is to establish a link or friendship with one or two colleagues in an organization. The success of the Board of Deputies from 1985 onwards was in part due to a strong bond between the President (Dr. Lionel Kopelowitz), the Treasurer (Jeffrey Pinnick) and myself, as Senior Vice President – a bond that continues to this day.

Serving in organisations with a strong human or caring objective demands sensitivity and commitment. Take the work and research undertaken in the area of autism, as an example. I have worked with people who daily, even hourly, remind me of the determination and love to support and encourage a child within the family however difficult the circumstances.

My work in the Zionist Federation was helped by an energetic young man, Alan Aziz, who helped to develop the organisation as he progressed. In consequence he introduced successive organisational teams of young people to our work and trained them with similar motivation and endeavour. Certainly one of the best professionals I have met in community and social care.

An odd ball incident concerned Victoria Beckham. I wrote a weekly feature commentary on social affairs for a modest paper circulated in the north of England amongst Jewish families. There was a minor reference to a sports charity and Victoria Beckham. It was certainly not directed at her but she felt slighted. An apology was given. I could have challenged the quotation but the editor had no wish to stand up to the celebrity in court and so he agreed to pay her demand for £2,000 compensation.

On a religious level, as a Jew one can be fully in tune with what our religion expects in commitment and ritual but I also look outside theology to assess the influences on the Jewish religion and others. Peter Berger, the American sociologist, explained our ability to reframe painful situations in such a way that we can find hope and humour, highlighting the human capacity to find such outlets even in the depths of suffering. Is it simplistic for Jews, Christians and Muslims to accept that there is within our spirit "something beyond" which includes humour and hope? Something for future bridges to be built upon?

Berger also argues in "A Rumour of Angels" for a many-sided conversation among sociologists, philosophers and anthropologists and theologists which could help to relieve some of the despair surrounding contemporary violence and intolerance in society.

Hope is critical. A concept I found most readily on my several visits to the Yad Vashem memorial in Jerusalem and also at the site of the extermination camp at Auchwitz. It is immensely difficult to be positive on such visits, certainly not on a first visit. Of the times I have been with multi-faith groups, with two of my children, Natasha and Josh, and I have been there alone. The first time I was there I had the awful feeling of isolation to convince myself it was not a bad dream, as the sunlight shone on the huts of extermination.

The destruction of humanity is utterly cruel and yet I was convinced of the hopefulness of life when following long conversations with one of the great leaders of survival Ben Helfgott. In a related experience Pope Francis also stressed such feelings when he visited Yad Vashem in 2014. He said the shoah was a momentous place in the human experience, not to be forgotten.

In recent years, the term Kindertransport has been bandied about in a lazy way, as Alison Pearson noted in the Daily Telegraph (Jan 31, 2016) "I have much sympathy with the view as many of the national services to recognise the Holocaust by arranging links with other areas of conflict yet to my mind the plight of Syrian refugees, however tragic, is not on a par with Jews fleeing the Nazis. From all I have seen and witnessed the Nazis deported the extended family where the strong were sorted from the weak and the young and the old people gassed."

Education can ensure that what we see and hear it is not a lost experience. The wish to remind future generations of the process of learning and understanding the holocaust has taken root and will not be lost, as shown in July 2014 when a remarkable gathering took place in Jerusalem of over 450 educators from 50 countries including China, Poland Argentina, Canada, Namibia, Venezuela, Greece and Spain. They gathered at Yad Vashem for the ninth International Conference on Holocaust Education. With the aim of investigating the roles of the survivor, the conference was organised into three main sections; the purpose of Holocaust documentation on the part of the first and second generations; how the events of the Shoah continue to find significance in the lives of those born afterwards; and the future of Holocaust education and remembrance among the youth of today – and tomorrow.

Neither the scale of the gathering nor the commitment of the education was in doubt. Perhaps it goes some way in answering Jews who question whether the lessons have been truly learnt when they see and hear expressions of anti-Semitism and incidents against Jews in their neighbourhoods throughout Europe.

I am under no illusions. I know that there are many expressions of hate directed against Jews and the religion. A distinguished Jew, Natan Sharansky now chairman of the Jewish Agency forecasts even more discrimination and attacks against Jews in Europe. He writes in the Jerusalem Post (15th August 2014) "Europe has become very intolerant of identities in a multicultural and post-nationalist environment" and that as a result Jews were caught in the middle of such a conflict.

"This new anti-Semitism is very connected to Israel – demonization and double standards – and is now so deep in the core of European political and intellectual leaders that practically every Jew is being asked to choose between being loyal to Israel and loyal to Europe," he wrote.

A consistent theme of my life has been to challenge racism and, if possible, to mitigate the excesses of inhumanity. I feel certain that many Jews and Christians have been saddened by the outbreak of Neo-Nazism. Prior to this I raised a number of issues in an address to the first annual Roots Conference on the Jewish experience and racism over 25 years. I noted that whilst many minority groups were being integrated in British society including Jews, many of the new recent arrivals often felt under threat.

It is a concern shared by many Asian families with whom I have spoken. Social pressures of modern society strains the family unit in general but it is even more frustrating amongst minority groups.

Of course there were many Christians who did speak out against such dangers through organisations of hope like the Inter-Faith Forum but I recognise that a formal structure alone cannot change attitudes and deep prejudices. In turn, it demands an understanding and a willingness to admit that such prejudices do exist.

The following letters seem to highlight the difficulties of addressing the subtle manifestation of the issues raised.

(a) While enduring the lengthy queue at Eastbourne's central post office this week, my patience was shared by a gentleman and his young daughter. Having lived in Israel for a while I recognised them as orthodox Jews, but what struck me – for the first time in this country – was that this man had felt it necessary to mask his appearance. His skull cap was hidden under a cap while his 'payot' (long side curls) were twisted behind his ears and tucked underneath.

We have reached a new low in Britain when citizens of any religious minority fear identification in a public place. Anne March, Eastbourne, E Sussex

(b) Sir, Growing anti-Semitism is another unforeseen consequence of Europe's departure from Christianity.

Notwithstanding certain times and places, Christianity has offered protection to jews and Judaism over the centuries due to shared scriptures, theology and ethics. Proactive atheistic campaigning to destroy the Judaeo-Christian basis of European society will continue to increase Jewish vulnerability.

Into the spiritual vacuum has stepped Islam with its specific creedal anti-Semitism. As the prophet Jeremiah said. "Peace, peace, they say, when there is no peace".

The Rev Dr Robert Anderson, Blackburn, Lancs.

Perhaps this last is true of Islamic fundamentalism only, but in just two letters from the Times from different stand points, we can see how Jews are reacting to anti-Semitic attacks in direct ways. Despite being simple examples the letters show that in everyday life the Jew must be on the alert and many will relate this to the early experiences of Jews living under threat elsewhere in the 1930s. The second letter (b) is equally as cautionary and is quite explicit.

For Jews the attacks are quite worrying and organised as reported by Hugo Rifkind on the disturbances in France on synagogues and shops, "Most of all never before have I felt that attitudes towards Jews in Europe – and even albeit less so, in Britain – could grow far, far worse before a whole swathe of supposedly progressive thought was even prepared to notice. It is not a nice feeling this last one.

People of all faiths need to be reminded of these concerns at present felt and experienced by Jews. David Nirenberg ("Anti-Judaism") 2013 wonders how much "reminding" is necessary. "Hostility to Judaism is not the product of occasional historical conjunctives, economic crises or far right political victories. Rather it is a constituent element of our culture and one of its critical roots."

It is troubling for many Jews to accept this as they are confronted with the growing number of anti-Semitic incidents reported by the Community Security Trust in Britain and similar bodies in France and the United States. But as Nirenberg says to confine anti-Judaism in the margins of our culture can be dangerously complacent.

Lord Jonathan Sacks points to an equally troubling conclusion:

"The new antisemitism is different from the old. In the past Jews were hated for their religion then for their race. Today they are hated for their nation state. But it was not long before I saw how seamlessly the old and new hatreds meshed".

A different strategy to deal with the increasing number of anti-Semitic incidents is called for. Hitherto each slur or abuse is challenged on a one-to-one basis. It is essential that we respond to any attack as racist.

One of the lessons of the Stockholm international forum, the largest conference devoted to the issues of prejudice, was that we shall, as Jews, need to overcome prejudice by forming the widest possible alliances. At that conference and since I have urged that Jews and other minorities need to work together to ensure that we are not isolated in our response whenever the charge is anti-Semitic or anti-black. Just as the anti-Semitic oppositions have forged links together we should make it clear that Jews do not stand alone.

Some will deny the proposition. Yet in my life and experience, I have seen much that confirms the concerns of Nirenberg and Sacks. All who can oppose racism should not be daunted. There is much to do in our lifetime. For my part I will continue to believe in, and raise awareness of, the simple fact that hatred towards the Jews never stops there.

A POSTSCRIPT

In my experience and research over the past few years, I have often been asked to go further in my analysis and forecast on the issues arising from the violent nature of our society and the emergence of the many facets of terrorism. What is the likely future for the democratic world is put to me in many forums? With that in mind I have added this postscript. It is not the book's conclusion but perhaps an overview of my experience both useful and useless.

Let me get one reflection out of the way. It almost seems that our political leaders appear not to be able to trust their various electorates on issues such as the growth and the hazard of terrorism, and its threat to their very lifestyle. Yes the political leadership did react with much compassion but no more. This has been very evident in all the terrorist acts over the past three years.

Should anyone doubt this proposition consider the debates and time and space devoted to these issues in recent elections and in particular the British 2015 General Election? The repeated issues and confrontations between parties invariably dwelt on economic shortfall or the number of houses to be built or failed to be built. Yet the international ramifications of conflict and terrorism in every part of the world is also our concern, thus our failure to understand the wider consequences could be tragically immediate. Consider the dangers within Britain as young men and women have opted to join the various terrorist groups in Syria having been indoctrinated here whether in schools, colleges or mosques and other security services. There is now an admission by government ministers as to how difficult it will be to monitor the numbers involved.

I have mentioned the failure of governments to act far more strongly than hitherto against those who generate hatred and violence. We should constantly emphasise the seriousness of the plight of those who live alongside the mighty and the powerful.

"Abderrahmane Sissako, the respected African film Director, made this very point and continues to do so in his films.

"We live in a world where suffering only seems to exist if it touches someone who looks like us. When someone slaughters (American journalist) James Foley or an Englishman or a Frenchman, there is an outcry. I too am enraged by such killings but those same butchers are each and every day slaughtering a great many other people and amputating the limbs of a great many others but those victims are not mentioned because of our indifference to people who do not resemble us. The world behaves as if these events have only been happening in recent months but that is not true. They have been happening for a long time."

We should not be indifferent to the suffering of others as I have stressed here many times, it can reach and affect us too.

I have attempted in my writings and lectures over time to alert the public to some of these risks and whilst there is some modest optimism, we seem unable to counter the consequences of conflict in regimes or settlers' feuds in, say, the Ukraine or the Middle East. To be alert and informed must be accepted as a serious undertaking.

The confusion over just what constitutes terrorism stems from the fact that every sovereign state reserves for itself the political and legal authority to define terrorism in the context of its domestic and foreign affairs. Governments speak with a bewildering variety of voices on the subject to terrorism. The United States is a case in point.

In the US federal system each state determines what constitutes an offence under its criminal or penal code. States have generally defined terrorism as a crime, thus ending the need for the use of specific statutes covering other selected criminal acts that are identified as terrorism. For instance, the Arkansas Criminal Code states that "a person commits the offence of terroristic threatening if with the purpose of terrorizing another person, he threatens to cause death or serious physical injury or substantial property damage to another person." In Britain and in other European countries, separate authorities deal with the various aspects of terrorism whether it is victim compensation, street terrorism, the threats to national security or ecological terrorism.

Over the past 30 years, the US Congress has held numerous hearings, considered bills, adopted resolutions and passed laws on terrorism. A comprehensive working definition that can address the different forms of terrorist attacks has not emerged from Congress thus far. Other countries such as the United Kingdom have adopted an evolutionary definition of terrorism.

The changes are likely within the course of the next few years. At present it is somewhat ambiguous.

International organisations, such as the United Nations, have also failed for decades to agree on a common definition.

We have also witnessed the violence of state sponsored terrorism which is more difficult to control because the use of state apparatus makes it that much easier for groups to conduct their operations and escape the clutches of the law. They can manipulate the law. Cross-border terrorism is often supported and sponsored by the intelligence agencies of the neighbouring countries. The international community must engage on a steep learning curve and act upon information about the make-up and travel intentions of terrorist groups. Britain and the United States already share such information.

In reviewing the nature of violence we must stress that terrorism is not a synonym for violence in general. Terrorism is a special kind of violence.

In Central America for instance, terrorism is used in conjunction with rural guerrilla warfare and with economic and political warfare in an all-out bid to topple governments but in Western Europe, which has experienced about 40% of all international terrorist incidents annually, terrorism is usually not accompanied by a wider insurgency but this percentage is increasing.

The sheer vulnerability of modern society, the ease of transferring sophisticated weaponry around the world, the ambivalent responses of many governments to attacks of terrorism and the complex structure of terrorist cells have all contributed to the success of world terrorism. Notwithstanding the fact that many serious attempts have been anticipated and prevented, we continue to face considerable danger at every level of civilisation as we know it.

The great danger as I see it in the next decade is a war by long range. Iran's nuclear weapons capability has raised that likelihood of such conflict. The answer is to waken the world's public interest. In Britain an even greater CND campaign that is even more determined than in the past along with an improvement and openness of our intelligence services is called for. More needs to be done to give a consistent message to the public in Britain on the likelihood of terrorist activity and its dangers. The PR success of the Falklands war was due to in some part to the daily press commentary surrounding events and developments and the sure touch of the presenter. What we have witnessed in Britain is a number of senior Ministers of State giving their own version or interpretations of the terrorist threat rather than a co-ordinated approach.

All this is a bottom line to safeguard and protect people everywhere. The consequences for Britain and the West have much to contribute in ensuring a continuation of the democratic way of life.

CAMEO FROM THE PAST

Arriving in London from Liverpool in the 1950s the author wrote a number of humorous articles about East London characters. Mr Plutnik was one of his most successful creations and read widely.

PLUTNIK

I first met Solomon Plutnik in our local sub-post office, one of those overcrowded, inefficient, dual-purpose shops which smelt of mail bags and ethnic foods. It was just before Christmas and the place was packed with people drawing out money and sending parcels to complicated places. There was a loud argument going on at the counter about which country Czechoslovakia was in and I was standing at the back considering how many friends I would lose if I sent all my Christmas cards without stamps. I had noticed this peculiar-looking old man peering at me and was thinking what to say if he asked me for money, when he came up to me and asked in mumbled, rapid Yiddish, if I could help him with his pools. I said that I would be delighted to, except I had no idea how to set about it and I was a very unlucky person with gambling. He assured me there was nothing to it. He did a 'perm', plan XYZ, 6d per line but he couldn't write to save his life. Normally the "Postmaster General" filled it in for him but she was too busy today and anyway he felt she cheated him, 'the dirty bastard', so would I please help an old man and maybe a cup of tea at the café next door?

Only a movie-camera could do justice to Mr. Plutnik. He said he was eighty-three, but it was difficult to tell if this was true because he had the kind of face and bearing that could have been anything over sixty. I remember he once showed me a photograph of himself when young and he looked exactly like he does now.

He was about four feet high: His head was large and completely hairless. His chin was pointed and he had a long, broad nose and small blinking eyes that hardly ever looked at you. Whether he was fat or thin it was impossible to tell owing to his extraordinary 'costumes' in which he was always wrapped. I say 'costumes' because he never wore clothes in the ordinary sense. Apart from his ties, I shouldn't think he had ever bought a garment especially meant for him. If he did buy anything, it was second-hand stuff from the stalls in the market, but mostly he just asked the people he knew to give him whatever he needed, regardless of size or anything else provided it was colourful and warm. With his ties, however, he was very careful, selecting them after weeks of inner debate and budgeting. His favourite colour was yellow and his best tie, which he wore for weighty occasions such as dead-watching and my son's "bris" was a brilliant "daffodil" embossed with a red emblem proclaiming "Rock 'n Roll". He always wore a hat and a long and cherished Crombie overcoat which touched the floor; and whatever the weather conditions, he carried a rolled umbrella. In short, he resembled an evil old elf disguised as a City gent in mid-winter.

On the day on which I first agreed to help him to fill in his pools coupon he was wearing his usual outer layer but with the addition of white spats: He also carried a cheap briefcase from which he had removed the handle, replacing it with one made out of a yellow sock. Underneath I discovered he was wearing a suit given him by one of the counter-hands in the post office who must have been at least seven foot tall. This was one of Mr. Plutnik's 'ploys'; To show that you were the only person kind enough to give him your cast-offs when he knew he would see you, he always wore something you had given him.

I lived nearby and as I did not want to display my ignorance of football pools to the crowd in the post office and was having a feud with the café next door, I decided to ask Mr. Plutnik to have a cup of tea in our flat. He accepted this suggestion with both alacrity and bad grace.

I looked at his muddy size – 10 shoes and decided we would do his pools in the kitchen. The kitchen had a yellow-tiled floor which filled Mr. Plutnik with delight and caused him to shuffle all over it for ten minutes. I thought how my wife would come home from solving people's problems all day and think I'd been entertaining Man Friday. Ever afterwards the kitchen was

Mr Plutnik's favourite room and it was only after some argument that we could ever persuade him to sit anywhere else.

Mr Plutnik spoke only Yiddish, apart from phrases like 'permutation' and 'silly bugger'. We had been conversing in Yiddish from the moment we met, when he suddenly turned on me and said (in Yiddish): "Do you speak Yiddish?"

"Well, of course, I do. What do you think we've been talking in up till now?"

"Are you a Yeshiva Bocha (strict religious student)?"

"If I was a Yeshiva Bocha, would I be likely to be doing your pools"?

He still looked suspicious. I could think of no reason for his ridiculous assumption than that he had seen that my wife and I possessed a great number of books.

He undid his brief case, which he had been clutching to himself as if it contained the Queen's Speech and fumbling, took from it about a hundred old football coupons and the Yiddish newspaper. It took a long time to fish out the current coupon, together with the instructions for his permutation and his postal order, so I was able to find out a bit more about him. I noticed that he actually lived up in Spitalfields, which was easily two miles away.

"You come a long way to get your postal order, don't you?"

"No, because I come here anyway to go to the Mission."

"What Mission?"

"The one over the road where they give you cash and tell you about Jesus. Every Thursday afternoon. And at Chanuka and Pesach you get a present and wine. In the summer they take me and the missus to Vestcliff for one day. They gave me this overcoat."

He gradually disclosed to me the shameful racket in which all the old Jewish men in the area were involved. The Mission was an organisation set up for the purpose of converting repentant Jews to Christianity. On first seeing the light the convert was given two pounds, then every Easter and Christmas he received 7/6d and a gift of clothes plus a day's outing in the summer with all the other converts. Every Thursday afternoon the flock would meet to hear the Gospel and to eat a sandwich and drink a cup of tea. Mr Plutnik thought it was a wonderful idea, fulfilling a crying need in the neighbourhood, namely, what to do on Thursday afternoons and where to get more clothes. He himself had been "converted" two years previously and was one of the Mission's most faithful followers. He was very impressed with the Jesus story which he had evidently not heard before, for he would relate various incidents to me as if they were current affairs.

"Do you know what Jesus has done today? There were all these people listening to him on a mountain and there were only five loaves and two fishes for them to eat so do you know what he did? He turned them into thousands. Enough for all. He's a marvellous person – a Yiddisher fella!"

On that first occasion I asked him if he believed in Jesus.

"Believe in him? What's believe in him?"

"Well – er – are you now a Christian, a goy?"

"What's this you're saying, am I a goy? Would I be speaking in Yiddish if I am a goy?"

"Well, do you go to synagogue now-a-days?"

"Of course I go. I have to. I'm a minyan man. They pay me 2/6d for Shabbas and more for Yom Taven (holy days). If I'm lucky, I earn a few pounds dead watching. My missus too. She doesn't care. It's a few pounds."

I suppose Mr. Plutnik was what you'd call playing the religious field.

I eventually completed his coupon and offered to keep the copy so that I could check it for him but he said he wanted to keep it himself so that when they came to give him his cheque the following Monday morning he would have proof of his coupon's validity.

He came every Thursday after that, and then he came one Sunday as my wife was serving our lunch. So we laid another place and divided up the food and my wife gave me a look which said that Sunday was the only day we had to ourselves and on which we had lunch at 4pm and she hoped this wasn't going to be a regular thing.

The following Sunday when I opened the door to him, he was wearing his Yarmulka.

'I don't like to eat bare-headed," he said.

Printed in the United States
By Bookmasters